The Solo Video Journalist

The Solo Video Journalist, now in its second edition, offers a comprehensive overview of the solo video reporting process from start to finish.

Drawing from years of professional experience in the field, the author covers all aspects of multimedia journalism, from planning for a segment, to dressing appropriately for multiple roles, to conducting interviews, and editing. The book contains interviews with more than a dozen top storytellers from around the United States and offers practical advice for how to succeed in a growing media field. New to this edition are Career Chronicles – chapters that detail the career paths possible for modern journalists – and a fully updated chapter on the importance of building a digital and social media presence.

This book is an excellent resource for students learning skills in broadcast, multimedia, backpack, and television journalism, as well as for early-career professionals looking for a back-pocket resource in solo video journalism.

Matt Pearl has worked in local television news for nearly two decades and is regarded as one of the top multimedia journalists in the country. He received his degree at Northwestern University with a BS in Journalism, and an MFA degree in Narrative Media from the University of Georgia, and has since gone on to win numerous awards for his work, including dozens of regional Emmys. Currently, he is a news reporter for WXIA-TV in Atlanta, Georgia, a position he has held since 2009. He has worked at various news stations and spoken at conferences about being a multimedia journalist. He has been named the national Solo Video Journalist of the Year multiple times by the National Press Photographers Association (NPPA).

The Solo Video Journalist

Doing It All and Doing It Well in TV Multimedia Journalism

Second Edition

MATT PEARL

Routledge
Taylor & Francis Group

NEW YORK AND LONDON

Second edition published 2020
by Routledge
52 Vanderbilt Avenue, New York, NY 10017

and by Routledge
2 Park Square, Milton Park, Abingdon, Oxon, OX14 4RN

Routledge is an imprint of the Taylor & Francis Group, an informa business

First edition published by Routledge 2017

Library of Congress Cataloging-in-Publication Data
A catalog record has been requested for this book

ISBN: 978-0-367-42997-3 (hbk)
ISBN: 978-0-367-43621-6 (pbk)
ISBN: 978-1-003-00464-6 (ebk)

Typeset in Dante and Avenir
by Swales & Willis, Exeter, Devon, UK

To Richard Schwarzlose, who always pushed me to think big

Contents

Foreword

I've been thinking a lot lately about stories. Mostly my dad's.

Andy Huppert was the first storyteller in my life. Growing up, as he did, in a three-bedroom farmhouse with 12 brothers and sisters, he was blessed with a wealth of material.

But it was more than his material. It was what he did with it.

Glee is the word that comes to mind. No one enjoyed telling a story more than my father. His eyes would light up as his laughter bubbled over, recounting his misadventures with schoolmates who seemed always to be nicknamed for their physical characteristics. It was a less sensitive time, when Chub, Stump, and Fats ruled the schoolyard, and decades later my dairy farmer father was still milking it for all it was worth.

I've been thinking a lot lately about my father's stories as I see him hunched, silently, in that powerlift recliner. If only he could tell me one of his stories now.

PSP – progressive supranuclear palsy – is a terrible disease. Google it some-time, and then pray no one you love is ever caught in its clutches.

Those afflicted gradually lose control of their muscles and, just as cruelly, their ability to communicate. My father's brain is still sharp, but his stories are now locked inside.

ALS will forever be associated with Lou Gehrig. In my mind, PSP is named Andy Huppert.

I've been thinking a lot lately about stories – the way they inform, entertain, and ultimately define us. And this is key: as much as any package wrapped up in birthday paper, stories are a gift to both the receiver and the giver.

As journalists we are endowed with that gift. We draw a paycheck for the very act that brought my father his greatest joy.

Matt Pearl has written an excellent guidebook for sharing stories in a changing media environment. Matt is part of a new generation of video storytellers breaking the mold and telling stories, solo, with a new set of tools. Yet Matt and others like him continue to draw on storytelling techniques that preceded my father, his father, and a hundred fathers before them.

From cavemen to Spielberg, the best among us have always had the ability to make an audience lean in, not quite sure where the story is going, but anticipating the next development on the shared journey.

As you think about stories – those you give, those you receive, and those you'll find on these pages – savor the privilege that is storytelling. My father made the most of his every opportunity to light up a room.

Study the lessons Matt has shared, hone your skills – and go light up some rooms.

Boyd Huppert, KARE TV

Preface to the Second Edition

I didn't expect this so soon.

I had hoped to one day write a second edition of *The Solo Video Journalist* but didn't imagine, less than three years after its initial publication, being asked to do so. When the e-mail came through, I first wondered: Had enough changed? Was three years enough time to substantially alter the world of solo video journalism? A few minutes of thought brought the obvious conclusion: Yes. Three years had brought change aplenty.

Much of that change has been welcome, starting with the expansion of opportunities. Digital-first outlets regularly hire do-it-all reporters to produce short-form features and long-form documentaries. Many young storytellers forgo the traditional career path – start in a small broadcast market and keep jumping until you reach a large one – and instead pitch freelance pieces they can produce themselves. These stories don't look like local news. They break the rules, take their time, and benefit from the expanded space of the digital realm.

The technology has also leaped forward. Smartphones have housed cameras for nearly a decade, but those cameras now shoot 4K video on devices with enough storage and editing software to enable high-quality video production. DSLR and mirrorless cameras have become commonplace in large local newsrooms, as have post-production sweeteners like Adobe After Effects and Photoshop. Today's solo video journalists shoot with smaller cameras, edit on effects-laden software like Premiere and Edius, and send stories from the field through hotspot-connected laptops. All of this enables and empowers us to produce stronger work. The ceiling for our potential keeps rising.

Finally, managers have always encouraged solo video journalists to develop a digital presence. Now they demand it. Reporters don't just shoot and edit stories for air; they write them for the web and post numerous times a day on social media. Instead of finding time for digital, they prioritize it.

The second edition of *The Solo Video Journalist* addresses these evolutions. Here's what's new:

- *Expansive advice on social media*: Rather than covering social media and the web with a brief chapter toward the back, I have rewritten the chapter entirely, updated it with new interviews and guidance, and moved it to the book's opening section.
- *Career Chronicles*: When I entered the industry in the mid-2000s, I saw few stable career paths in video journalism outside of local TV news. In these chapters, I speak with several solo video journalists who have found fulfilling roles in uncommon places, or used their solo status to catalyze moves to more traditional roles.
- *The MMJ Survey*: For too long, the job of a solo video journalist has been viewed and defined in its simplest terms … at least by those who have never worked as one. I recently surveyed nearly 100 do-it-all reporters about how they view their role. This chapter explores their responses – and the revelations that affect everyone in the industry.

Perhaps the book's most significant update comes from not its content but those providing it. While I am extremely proud of the original edition, I failed to find a diverse enough group of speakers to reflect the make-up of today's working one-person crews. Almost all of my interviews featured white men in broadcast news. Not this time. I have quadrupled the representation of minority journalists, spoken with storytellers across platforms with different paths to the field, and interviewed an equal number of female and male solo reporters. The second edition is stronger because of this. Greater diversity of background leads to greater diversity of thought, and I am proud to have connected with so many dynamic journalists with important perspectives.

Three years has indeed brought change. But the heart of storytelling stands firm. In the process of compiling the new edition, I retyped each word from the original and analyzed as I went. I was delighted to see how well the core chapters held up. The techniques discussed for shooting, interviewing, writing, and editing remain relevant and effective. The advice about time management – and its importance for enabling deeper thought about one's stories – remains critical. While our gear gets smaller and our responsibilities grow larger, our journalistic foundations endure.

So does our necessity.

This industry needs passionate storytellers who aim to impact their communities. Increasingly, those storytellers work alone. We must raise our voices and maximize our talents. We must be leaders and influencers. We must value what we do.

And, as I have done in updating this book, we must always evolve, improve, and stride forward.

Acknowledgments

I first contemplated authoring a book on solo video journalism while preparing to propose to my girlfriend.

I wrote the majority of the original manuscript in the months after getting married. (I even agreed to a two-week laptop break while we took our honeymoon.)

And I typed these acknowledgments for the second edition of *The Solo Video Journalist* as the father of a 21-month-old daughter, my wife six months pregnant with our second.

Our worlds don't stop. Any significant achievement in our careers will almost surely coincide with a significant time in our lives, because every time in our lives is significant. Perhaps that sounds daunting. But I think it's beautiful. When you do something you love – and put your heart and effort into making it great – you fulfill your life in a meaningful way.

I believe in journalism and storytelling as fulfilling paths. But I also understand the toll they exact. I have witnessed too many colleagues pursue the field, become turned off by its increasingly formidable demands – particularly as solo video journalists – and decide it's not worth the investment. I fully understand.

I wrote *The Solo Video Journalist* to empower journalists to invest further. Perhaps, as soloists, we work alone, but that's even greater reason to seek community. We need it in our careers, from colleagues who share our experiences, provide instructive feedback, and breathe the highs and lows of our profession. We need it in our lives, from friends and family who encourage our growth, champion our achievements, and satisfy the many desires that can't be found through a camera and microphone.

It's only fitting I acknowledge my community. I couldn't have produced this book without it.

I must thank the Taylor & Francis group and Routledge imprint for its continued interest and enthusiasm, with special thanks to Margaret Farrelly, Priscille Biehlmann, Ross Wagenhofer, Nicole Salazar, Christopher Taylor, Bonita Glanville-Morris, Deirdre Byrne, and Linda Bathgate. I must also acknowledge the team at Swales & Willis for its work on production, including Julian Webb, Colin Morgan, and particularly copy-editor Simon Barraclough for his thorough and thoughtful examination of the words you're reading. My bosses at TEGNA and WXIA-TV, particularly my news director Jennifer Rigby, have always allowed me to explore my storytelling passions, even beyond the TV newsroom. Fellow journalists Wayne Freedman, Sean Moody, Stace Hall, and Bill Liss lent advice and insights; my friend Nicole Leffer provided her gift for photography. And before I had written a single page, my longtime friend Adam Levine helped guide me through my proposal.

This book is bolstered by the journalists interviewed within it. Heidi Wigdahl, Anne Herbst, Mitch Pittman, Forrest Sanders, and Peter Rosen all granted me their time; Greg Bledsoe, Joe Little, and Ted Land even did so in person. Jon Shirek has always inspired me in the WXIA newsroom, and he was an invaluable resource throughout the project. I'm saddened I cannot include Mike Castellucci and Mike McCarthy in this edition, but I appreciate their initial contributions and admire each greatly. I'm excited to welcome new voices and perspectives to the second edition: Blayne Alexander, Emily Kassie, Sarah Blake Morgan, Dougal Shaw, Tiffany Liou, Neima Abdulahi, and Paige Pauroso. Finally, I am honored that Boyd Huppert agreed to both be interviewed and write the foreword. I cannot think of anyone more appropriate to introduce a book about telling stories.

In the time between the 1st edition and this one, I started and completed grad school. I received my MFA in Narrative Media from the Grady College of Journalism at the University of Georgia, and I was guided by accomplished professionals who alchemize words into opulent images. They weren't directly involved with this book, but my mentors at UGA – particularly Valerie Boyd, Lolis Eric Elie, and John T. Edge – helped raise my writing to new heights.

I must acknowledge the mentors in my career who could never have known their support would lead to a book: Dan Moran of East Brunswick High School, Richard Schwarzlose of Northwestern University, Tedd O'Connell of KMEG-TV, and Ellen Crooke of everywhere since. You have each guided me in different ways, but more than that you have always stoked, supported, and championed my passion.

Above all, I want to thank the people in my life for whom my gratitude and love will forever shine. My grandfather, Poppy, is a beaming light and unconditional cheerleader. My sister, Jessica, is a beautiful and dynamic soul who impresses me with her desire to imbue life with meaning. My mother, Meri, is the calming, loving voice on the other end of the phone. My father, Marc, is my eternal role model, who has checked my work from kindergarten all the way through this book.

Finally, my wife, Karen, is the smile that brightens my every day, and my daughters, Olivia and Isla, are the source of my deepest responsibility and purest joy. I could not imagine writing this book, or living my life, without them.

Introduction

I am a Solo Video Journalist

Figure 0.1

Credit: Luke Carter

"Where's your photographer?"

This is the question I hear most when meeting someone I am about to interview.

I have worked as a television journalist for nearly two decades, won several of the industry's highest honors, and covered some of the world's most momentous events. But when I show up at someone's doorstep or office with a camera in one hand, tripod in the other, and a backpack on my shoulders, I receive the same puzzled expression – the one that says, "Aren't you supposed to have someone else with you?"

I laugh it off, respond with a joke, and assure my interview subject that my role is perfectly common.

I am a solo video journalist.

And I have a great job.

Broadcast news has always appeared more glamorous on screen than in person, but perhaps no trend represents this more than the rise of the solo video journalist. The idea – at least, as a widespread concept – is still relatively new, and even my own industry cannot agree on what to call me. Many stations use the term "multimedia journalist" or "MMJ." Others say "one-man-band," "backpack journalist," or "do-it-all reporter." (You will see all these terms in this book.) On camera, I appear no different than my fellow reporters. Off camera, I juggle twice the responsibilities and apply far more physical effort, shooting and editing my own stories.

When I describe this to people outside the industry, they tend to respond with a mixture of awe and pity. They cannot believe such a job exists, where one person must possess such seemingly disparate skills. They occasionally say something like, "Well, I'm sure one day you won't have to do that anymore."

I bristle when I hear that … because I know two things:

First, solo video journalism is no longer a means to an end, a stepping stone until one gets that "real" reporting job. For many, it is a full-fledged career path that has led the way to groundbreaking, award-winning coverage.

Second, I have experienced opportunities, assignments, and successes in my career that I had never imagined, and I have received them largely because I do it all.

My journey in television news reflects the value of versatility. At my first job at KMEG-TV in Sioux City, Iowa, I served as a one-man sports department. I produced, shot, wrote, edited, and anchored two sportscasts a night. I then worked at WGRZ-TV in Buffalo, N.Y., starting as a sports reporter/producer and becoming a weekend sports anchor and weekday news reporter, known for long-form human-interest stories that captured people's attention. I began to reap the benefits of my solo status, winning four Regional Edward R. Murrow Awards and traveling alone to Denver to cover the 2008 Democratic National Convention. In 2009, I moved to Atlanta to work for WXIA-TV, where I achieved even greater success. In my first decade at the station, I earned 30 Southeast Emmy Awards in a wide range of categories, almost always competing against stories from traditional two-person crews. I was named, five times, the National Press Photographers Association's Solo Video Journalist of the Year.

I have also received extraordinary assignments. In 2010, my parent company, Gannett (now called TEGNA), was planning its coverage of the Winter Olympics in Vancouver and wanted to send as many reporters as possible. The company chose to use largely solo video journalists, who could produce the same amount of content for half the price. I was among the MMJs selected, and I spent a month in a foreign country reporting from one of the most watched events of the year and supplying stories to stations across America. Since then I have covered multiple Olympic Games (Figure 0.2), three Super Bowls, the World Series, and a presidential inauguration – almost always producing stories alone.

I am hardly the exception. Solo video journalists now occupy a substantial segment of TV newsrooms. The latest study from the RTDNA found that 93% of local network affiliates use them in some capacity, including 83% of affiliates in the top 25 markets. Among new hires in broadcast news departments, MMJs ranked second among all positions, surpassing anchors and producers. The only job more requested? Digital journalists (Papper, 2018). That's another new lane. The explosion of video online, from both television and digital outlets, provides opportunities and assignments for those who can do it all.

As the number of solo video journalists rises, so does the number of those in positions of power. At TEGNA alone, two one-time MMJs at my station have since taken jobs as news directors in medium-sized markets. Others have been promoted to positions with "Chief" at the front. The NPPA just handed the reins of its prestigious Advanced Storytelling Workshop to Anne Herbst, a one-time Solo Video Journalist of the Year. Fellow soloist Sarah Blake Morgan

Figure 0.2 Solo video journalism can take you to a different continent. In 2016 it took me to the Summer Olympics in Rio de Janeiro.

Credit: Matt Pearl

runs a Facebook group that launched in 2016 to empower female MMJs and now features thousands of members. One-person crews have won Peabody Awards, National Edward R. Murrow Awards, and hundreds of Emmys. We are an unstoppable force.

My message to aspiring reporters is this: Think of what you want to accomplish in your career, and understand you can likely do so as a solo video journalist. It does not need to be a stepping stone. It can be your entire path.

But it brings challenges. Becoming a talented MMJ requires learning a variety of seemingly divergent skill sets. The traits of a thorough reporter do not necessarily match those of a strong photographer. A one-person crew must also juggle numerous responsibilities and deal with a unique set of hurdles en route to producing a story.

Very few books discuss these challenges and provide a thorough overview of how to conquer them. Even fewer provide the perspective of present-day journalists, let alone MMJs themselves. The practice of solo video journalism, as popular as it has become, is still young enough that many teachers and authors do not quite know how to approach it. Aspiring reporters, too often, must figure it out on their own.

Enter this book.

Consider the next 183 pages a how-to guide for solo video journalism. I have drawn on my own experiences while picking the brains of some of the finest one-woman and one-man bands working today, and I have produced an easy-to-follow, comprehensive collection of tips and techniques for becoming a well-rounded, powerful storyteller.

The first part of the book deals with the importance of preparation. Chapter 1 focuses on planning: how to arrive at the station prepared, brainstorm a story, back-time your day, and wisely use what some might call "downtime." Chapter 2 discusses hair, make-up, and clothing, with advice on how to dress appropriately for both shooting and reporting. Chapter 3 talks about equipment, from lights and headphones to the camera itself. Chapter 4 looks at how to develop a digital presence and balance your on-air and online responsibilities.

Part II is entitled "In the Field" and dissects the story-gathering process. Chapter 5 covers the rules and guidelines for collecting footage, or B-roll. Chapter 6 provides advice for conducting interviews. Chapter 7 dives into the seemingly tricky maneuver of shooting your own stand-ups.

Part III focuses on putting it all together. Chapter 8 offers a deep dive into logging interviews and writing your story. Chapter 9 examines editing – a critical skill for any visual storyteller. Finally, the fourth and final section consists of chapters that provide advice for thinking big in the journalistic field.

In addition, I have included chapters throughout the book called "Career Chronicles," which focus on the various paths available to those who do it all. Some, like me, lean into their solo status and carve unique roles in the industry. Others use it as a springboard to more traditional jobs. These chapters combine with the others to provide a complete foundation for up-and-coming MMJs.

I decided to write this book because I believe in its importance. I have benefited so much from capitalizing on my role as a solo video journalist, and I wish to see others do the same. As you read these words and use their advice, I implore you to reach out to me with any questions or requests for critique. I can be reached via e-mail at mattpearlreports@gmail.com.

I wish you all the best as you begin, or continue, your journey.

Reference

Papper, B. (2018, April 16). "Research: TV News Employment Surpasses Newspapers" [Web Log Post]. Retrieved from www.rtdna.org/article/research_tv_news_ employment_surpasses_newspapers

Part I

Before the Story

Planning Your Day 1

Figure 1.1
Credit: Matt Pearl

I begin the first chapter of this book about journalism with an example from a similarly hallowed field:

Golf.

(Don't worry if you don't know much about golf. Neither do I.)

I spent countless hours during my mid-20s trying to master the sport, usually spending my midweek off days on the fairways of Buffalo's finest courses. (In Buffalo, "golf season" meant "mid-May to mid-September," which may explain why I never shot less than 20 over par.) I did not learn much, but I did pick up a piece of advice that applies perfectly to solo video journalism: "In chaotic environments, try to eliminate as many variables as possible."

In golf, the chaos exists because of the perfection required to succeed. Each swing features numerous elements beyond one's control – and thus numerous opportunities to make mistakes. Think of the many variables:

- The sun, or lack thereof
- Wind, rain, or any other type of weather
- One's view, which is never the same except at the start of a hole
- The placement of the pin on the green.

The swing itself creates even more anarchy, because once a golfer pulls back the club, he or she begins a continuous movement that will not stop until that club strikes the ball. If something feels a bit off – the speed of the backswing, the turn of the body, the height of the club at its apex – the golfer cannot stop mid-shot; he or she must adjust on the fly. This further unfolds the chaos and underscores what makes golf such an elusive game.

A wise golfer responds by establishing a pre-shot routine that seldom changes. When I played, I went through a mental checklist every time I approached the ball, inspecting everything from the width of my feet to the angle of my arms to the tightness of my grip. My mindset? Control all I could before the shot, realizing how little I could control once it began.

I never became a great golfer, but I have used that philosophy to become a much stronger solo video journalist.

Anyone can benefit from the critical skill of preparation, but MMJs require it. A solo video journalist, in a basic sense, consists of a single person filling two traditional jobs. This removes many of the luxuries reporters take for granted, such as:

- Looking up phone numbers and e-mail addresses while the photographer drives
- Posting on social media while the photographer shoots extra footage
- Taking photos with the phone while the photographer uses a camera.

It also adds a seemingly dizzying number of responsibilities – tasks that, in theory, deal more with housekeeping than reporting.

Consider the simple number of objects an MMJ must monitor. Start with the camera and everything that goes with it: batteries, lights, memory cards, lens cleaner, microphones, attachments, and, of course, the tripod. Then add all the traditional accessories of a reporter: a laptop (with all of its cords and chargers), notepads, make-up, and additional clothing, such as a suit jacket or winter coat.

Oh, and MMJs in many newsrooms are assigned their own vehicles. Try keeping track, amidst your regular workload, of oil checks and emissions inspections.

This is why it's so important to eliminate variables, and why I am using the opening chapter of this book to preach the dogma of time management. Journalism is chaotic enough, solo video journalism even more so. Make it slightly more manageable, and you stand a much better chance of telling the stories you and your viewers desire.

I learned how by watching one of my most impressive colleagues.

The first time I spoke with Jon Shirek, I had no idea I would, eight months later, become his coworker.

In 2008 I was nearing the end of my third year at WGRZ-TV in Buffalo; Jon was nearing his 30th year at WXIA-TV in Atlanta. Our stations shared a mutual owner, Gannett, which also held more than 90 daily newspapers. With a presidential election looming in November, Gannett's leaders wanted to bolster its coverage of the preceding political conventions, so they selected two TV multimedia journalists – one for each convention – to work exclusively for the newspapers, providing video stories and sound bites for the publications' web sites.

That's how Shirek (Figure 1.2) wound up traveling to the Republican National Convention to cover the nomination of Senator John McCain – and how I found myself on a plane to Denver for the Democratic National Convention and the nomination of the eventual president, Barack Obama.

It stands, to this day, among the most memorable assignments of my career ... and the most grueling. I worked more than 60 hours in four days, producing maybe a dozen stories and hauling at least 40 pounds of gear every day from my rental car to the workspace. By the time it ended, I was so exhausted I overslept the final morning and almost missed my flight home.

The DNC wrapped three days before the RNC began, and Shirek reached out to pick my brain about how everything had gone. He asked about the smoothness of the operation, the expectations from Gannett, and the workflow during such a crowded environment. He touched on everything

Figure 1.2 Jon Shirek.

I would expect from a seasoned, esteemed reporter. I left the conversation thinking, "This guy knows his stuff."

Turns out he had only worked as an MMJ for one month.

"I don't know why or how or what was behind all that," Shirek told me. "But for whatever reason, they wanted a one-man band to go and help out, so I said, 'I'm game. I'll go.'"

Shirek was hired as a reporter in Atlanta in 1980, working with photographers "who knew how to make every frame a Rembrandt," he says. That remained the case for nearly three decades, until the trend of backpack journalism made its way to the eighth largest market in the country. WXIA had already hired two MMJs, and its managers began asking several long-time reporters to make the transition. Shirek accepted the move but feared its impact on his performance. "I didn't have enough confidence in myself to be able to master it," he said. "I wasn't sure I could do the good work I wanted to do."

How did he cope? The same way he approached the RNC: by preparing himself.

"It was just a matter of doing it and figuring out how to set up the workflow, so to speak – to try to make it as easy as possible and not let yourself get in the way of what you were trying to do."

To watch Shirek today is to witness a composed professional amidst the newsroom commotion. He wields his solo status in ways that suit his skills, and he operates with a routine and workspace that give him room to focus on his daily stories.

He also knows the best way to win the day is to start your routine long before you receive your assignment.

Before You Start Your Workday

Here is the piece of advice that underlies virtually every element of time management:

Know yourself.

Know how much time you need to complete certain tasks. Know the ins and outs of your workflow, and know the equipment you require for each step. Know which tasks you will definitely remember when you are scrambling out the door, and know which ones you might potentially forget.

Then, develop a pre-workday routine that accounts for all of it.

A solo video journalist is, in essence, following two routines: a reporter's and a photographer's. Both are crucial – and likely being followed by your colleagues in more traditional positions.

On the reporting side, stay on top of the day's news and walk in the door with story ideas. This is sometimes tough for young journalists, especially those new to a market. The more quickly one can meet people and develop sources, and the more frequently one can check both traditional and social media for potential stories, the more prepared one will be for an assignment.

Few do this as well as Shirek. Admittedly, he starts with the advantage of experience, as both a journalist (nearly 50 years) and Atlantan (40 years). But every time I watch him at a pitch meeting, I marvel at the number of compelling, well-researched stories he submits. General assignment reporters usually receive assignments based on the news of the day or, sometimes, other people's pitches; they must then spend valuable time catching up on a story before they can work to advance it. Shirek, more times than not, gets to work on stories he developed himself, which gives him a valuable head start (Figure 1.3).

He does it with a strict routine.

"You look at all the newspapers around the area," Shirek says. "You scan (your Twitter feed) to see what everybody's up to. You think of good follow-ups to stories you did that can be advanced. By the time you get to the meeting, you can't wait for your turn to come up."

Figure 1.3 Shirek's famed reporter notebooks contain hundreds of ideas.
Credit: Matt Pearl

On the photography side, develop a system for your gear. Any journalist who has regularly operated a camera has, at some point, left for a shoot without a seemingly basic piece of equipment.

Forget to charge your batteries? You can't shoot your story.

Forget your memory card? You can't shoot your story.

Forget your camera? You get the idea.

I learned this the hard way at my first job. I had secured an interview with an official at the University of South Dakota, a 30-minute drive from my station in Sioux City, Iowa. Somewhere around minute 25 of that drive, I realized I had left the newsroom without a tape on which to record.

I will never forget the five stages of shame that followed.

First: Denial mixed with desperate hope. "Did I really forget a tape? Am I sure I didn't put one in the camera? I have to have another tape in this car somewhere, right?"

Second: Panic. "What am I going to do? Can I still get this story done? Do I actually have time to turn around, drive back to the station, pick up a tape (and hope no one notices my slunk-shouldered entrance and exit), and make this same trip all over again?"

Third: Calm realization. If you ask yourself the questions of Stage 2 and answer "No," then you head home, knowing you have made a massive and easily avoidable mistake. If you answer "Yes," as I did on this occasion, you breathe deeply and, for a moment, take comfort that you have not wasted your entire day … just a large chunk of it.

Fourth: The embarrassing walk-through. You follow all the steps from your earlier checklist of questions, all while notifying the bare minimum of people who need to be aware of your error. In this case, I informed the university official I would need to postpone our interview by an hour. I did not even try to invent a semi-believable excuse. I laid my humiliated head at his feet, and he thankfully gave me a pardon. Then I drove back to the station, got my new tape, and headed up to South Dakota a second time.

Fifth: Resolution. Perhaps you have heard the expression, "Making mistakes is OK; just don't make them twice." If so, you probably know what happened next: I got my act together and developed a system to ensure I would never experience this again. I had dodged disaster, but I knew I would not always be so fortunate.

These days I keep most of the essential items – camera, tripod, lights, and a spare battery and memory card – in my news vehicle. I also run through a daily mental checklist upon my arrival at work, gathering a charged camera battery, fresh AA batteries for my wireless microphones, and clean memory cards. I place them next to my laptop and grab them as I leave.

Shirek conducts his routine the night before.

"It's very simple," he told me while sitting at his cubicle. "I'm here with my laptop, and I copy over all the raw video I want to save. Then I clear the camera cards; I put the [previous day's] battery on charge; I put the camera cards back in the camera; I make sure the battery's charged on the camera; I make sure the lens is clean; and I make sure the batteries on the wireless microphone are full. And then I go home!"

Such a procedure can seem overly cautious and even tedious, especially if you complete your shift, as Shirek often does, close to midnight. But the next day, Shirek says, "You can jump in the car and go, and not give your equipment a second thought."

After You Receive Your Assignment

Well, maybe have a few second thoughts … but not about your equipment.

Once you learn your story assignment for a given day, you will feel tempted to head right out the door. You will want to make calls, set up interviews, and secure the first available time to meet someone in the field. You will sense your first deadline already creeping up, and you will not want to waste any time at the station when you could be on the road, en route to wherever you story will take you.

The impulse is understandable and sometimes unavoidable. A breaking news story or imminent press conference might demand your speedy departure, which you will be able to make because you have already gathered your gear and packed everything you need.

Most stories, though, come with a little leeway. In these cases, a solo video journalist's wisest move is to take a few minutes to simply think.

When I receive an assignment, I rarely hit the road right away. I sit at my computer, allot 5–10 minutes, and brainstorm my approach to that day's story. I ask myself the questions that will inform my thought process the rest of the way:

- Why does this story matter?
- What will compel my audience to watch?
- Who do I need to contact to ensure I tell a complete story?
- How can I approach the piece visually and creatively?
- Really, though: Why does this story matter?

Sometimes I get lucky and stumble on a potential line of script that could work for the piece. Mostly I walk away with something far more important: a plan.

"If you're in this line of work, everything fascinates you," Shirek says. "Sometimes it's just a matter of thinking in advance, 'What are the possible ways you could put this story together, based on what you know now and what you might know later?' If I've got a line that might work, I'll write it down so I don't forget it."

Perhaps the most important part of the brainstorming process is to back-time your day. I have heard this advice from countless colleagues in the business, and I have sworn by it throughout my career.

What is "back-timing?" It requires plotting out, either in your head or on your phone, how much time you require for each step of the storytelling process. This is where that "Know yourself" philosophy pays off.

For proof, I can point to the most famous story of my career.

In June 2014, I had just begun my sixth year at WXIA and I walked in on a Monday morning for my standard dayside shift. I attended the daily pitch meeting at 9:30 and left with my assignment at around 10:15. That story fell through, and for the next 30 minutes, I sat at my desk and scoured my feeds for a new one.

Then our assignment editor received a call: a man in Madison County, Ga. had spotted and rescued a baby crawling along the side of the highway.

Everyone's ears perked up.

I had, it seemed, received my new mission. But I suspected I would need to travel a long distance to cover it, and a quick search on Google Maps confirmed those fears:

Madison County was 90 minutes away.

I felt the impulse to head straight to the car, but I resisted. I instead went through my usual brainstorming process, and I thought seriously about how I would need to schedule my day. My story, I was told, would run during our 6 PM newscast, so I worked my way back and gave myself a series of deadlines:

- 11:15 AM: Depart for Madison County
- 12:45 PM: Arrive in Madison County; interview the main subject and shoot B-roll
- 1:45 PM: Leave the main subject and head to the sheriff's department for an interview
- 2:15 PM: Depart for Atlanta (and account for potential mid-afternoon traffic)
- 4 PM: Return to WXIA-TV headquarters
- 4:05 PM: Log my interviews
- 4:30 PM: Write my story
- 5 PM: Edit my story
- 5:45 PM: Send the complete package to the server for air
- 6 PM: Sit back and watch my story on television.

I now possessed a plan, and while it still seemed daunting, with little margin for error, I at least knew it could be done.

I then made the necessary calls, set up my interviews, and left for Madison County … but not before preparing for the most challenging part of my day: the drive.

As Shirek says: "On your way to the story, you're unable to be a reporter while you're driving. That's the weakest link in this whole MMJ chain, because you are so limited in what you can do."

He is right … mostly. You cannot perform many tasks from the driver's seat that a traditional reporter can do from the passenger's side, but you can handle them before you leave the building. Before I walk out the door, I write down any pertinent details and plug all necessary contact numbers into my phone. I spend several minutes on Google, research the latest information on my story, and make a list of anyone I might want to call from the road.

I also try to recognize the possibility that I will not get the chance that day to return to the newsroom. Live shots, breaking news, and a host of other hurdles can keep someone in the field all day, and an MMJ must prepare. Shirek loads his computer with "as much file video as I think I will need. I download stuff from the Internet, and I look for photographs on Getty Images. [Our station had a subscription.] I do everything I can to get what I need onto that laptop before I go."

With the Madison County story, I did not need to find any file video, because none existed. But I printed out directions and wrote down the names and numbers of my contacts, including the most critical one: Bryant Collins, the man who found the baby.

Then I headed to the car, for a 90-minute drive that made a giant impact.

While You Drive to Your Story

During my earliest years in the business, I frequently made a major mistake as soon as I sat behind the wheel:

I turned on the radio.

I raised the volume, flipped through my preset stations, and cruised the streets of Iowa listening to the biggest hits of 2003.

Here, for the record, were the biggest hits of 2003:

1. "In da Club" by 50 Cent
2. "Ignition (Remix)" by R. Kelly
3. "Get Busy" by Sean Paul
4. "Crazy in Love" by Beyonce feat. Jay-Z
5. "When I'm Gone" by Three Doors Down
6. "Unwell" by Matchbox 20
7. "Right Thurr" by Chingy ("Billboard Year-End Hot 100 singles of 2003," n.d.)

Look at this list again, and decide for yourself: did I truly need to hear that Sean Paul song for the 30th time? Or, perhaps, should I have focused more on my assignment?

At the time, I did not think I could accomplish much in the car. I treated it like the aforementioned weakest link, failing to realize that even the weakest link remains a vital part of the chain.

Shirek has transformed his car into his primary workspace. His glove compartment overflows with cords and chargers. He even keeps a digital audio recorder so that, after he collects his video, he can listen to interviews while he drives.

"I go through one or two a year," he says. "To me, it's just one of the tools."

I do not maintain as elaborate a setup, but I use my time in the car to continue the brainstorming process. I make additional phone calls and occasionally pre-interview my story's subjects. I think thematically about the assignment and try to determine which elements require the most attention. Sometimes my thoughts are those of a traditional reporter. During breaking news, for example, my first responsibility is to learn as much as I can about the 5 Ws (who, what, when, where, and why) of the situation. For other stories, like human-interest pieces or features, I find myself thinking more like a photographer. Shirek did so on a story where a Chick-fil-A employee had found a patron's wallet that had been sitting on the counter for 20 minutes. Shirek wanted to capture the moment when the patron went back to the restaurant to meet his Good Samaritan.

"So I'm thinking," he recalls: "I have one chance to show this man coming back to the restaurant and meeting the employee who found his money.' I'm thinking, 'Where is this going to happen? Is it going to happen inside? Is there going to be enough light? Will there be enough room? I won't be able to hear in a crowded restaurant, so I have to intercept this guy before he goes in.'"

Shirek made the interception, captured the moment, and produced a heartwarming feature.

In my case, I spent most of my drive to Madison County thinking about logistics. I knew I would not have much time in the field, and I did not want to waste any of it playing catch-up, so I made phone calls. I reached out to the sheriff to learn more details and tried to obtain an e-mail copy of the incident report. I contacted my producer and assignment editor to alert them of my progress.

I also placed one more call to Bryant Collins.

Back in the newsroom, I had spoken with Collins for a minute or two because I knew I needed to get out the door. I explained the time constraints and, after setting up his interview, asked if I could call from the car to learn more. When I rang back, we talked for 15 minutes about an array of subjects:

- I found out exactly what had happened: Collins was driving while at work as an auto repairman, and he could not believe his eyes when he saw a baby crawling by the side of the road, mere feet from the whizzing cars on the highway.
- I learned how he responded: Collins got out of his truck, picked up the little girl, and stayed for two hours – even after the police arrived – to keep her calm and safe.

- I determined how I would get my footage: Collins said I would have to catch him during work, which meant I could record him as he serviced a car. He also said he would be happy to take me to the location where he found the baby, which would enable me to shoot video and interview him at the scene.

I discovered something else: Collins had survived a checkered past. He referenced it several times during our phone call, and while I did not ask for specifics then, I did so later during our interview, when Collins again brought up the subject.

He then told me the detail that became the pivotal moment of my story.

Collins said he had served ten years in jail for manufacturing cocaine. He had pledged in prison to turn his life around, and he had done so, staying clean and sober since his release five years earlier. Had he not changed his ways, he told me, he never would have been able to save that child.

He seemed so grateful for all that had transpired, because it had led him to that moment.

I was stunned, and as I bid Collins farewell and continued on my checklist, I knew I had found the centerpiece of my script. I spent the drive home writing in my head, and I put together a story that went viral within minutes, receiving millions of views on my station's Facebook page. It even reached producers at NBC Nightly News, which aired a slightly edited version the following night.

This, of course, does not always happen. In fact, that kind of response rarely occurs. But much like Collins' actions years earlier had put him in a position to save someone's life, my preparation and time management had set me up for storytelling success.

After all, you can only somewhat control what happens during the golf swing. But you can fully control what happens before it.

Reference

"Billboard Year-End Hot 100 singles of 2003" (n.d.). *Wikipedia*. Retrieved March 6, 2016, from https://en.wikipedia.org/wiki/Billboard_Year-End_Hot_100_singles_of_2003

Looking the Part **2**

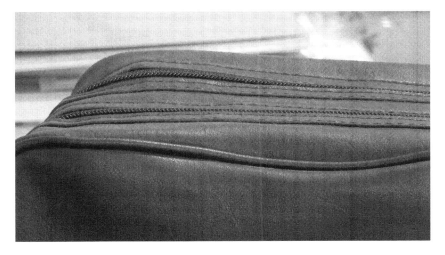

Figure 2.1

Credit: Matt Pearl

One of my most intimidating moments as a young journalist came when I received, in college, a crucial assignment:

I needed, for the first time, to buy make-up.

I was a sophomore at Northwestern University, and I had just signed up for my first class about television news. Our professor informed us we would be recording a newscast, and we would need to look our best on camera.

That meant wearing make-up – a topic about which I knew extremely little.

I didn't mind the idea. I had actually worn make-up several times: once when I performed in theater shows in high school, and once when, on the day of my bar mitzvah, I tried to hurdle over the side of a staircase and banged my nose into the railing. (My mother was not pleased.)

But I felt out of my element actually purchasing it … and would feel more so after my first experience.

My classmate and I walked into a suburban Chicago department store and went up to one of the make-up counters. We explained to the salespeople what we desired – products that would look good on camera for a newscast – and promptly received the most extreme of makeovers. The salespeople sat us down and applied seemingly everything in stock: eyeliner, eye shadow, blush, lip gloss, and whatever else they could fit on our faces. They did this while providing zero access to a mirror. At last they concluded and turned us around to show their work.

It was no Monet.

I have seen few people wear as much make-up as I displayed in that moment. I looked like a caricature, and I quickly reached for whatever towels and tissues I could find to wipe it all off. I had not wanted to learn about make-up in the first place; I saw it as a superficial and artificial element of life as a broadcast journalist. I left the experience as clueless as when it began, fearing I would permanently struggle with a far too difficult concept.

Turns out, it's actually pretty simple.

I learned soon after exactly what kind of make-up I would need and why. I found two products that were easy to apply and made me presentable – and, more importantly, freed me from worrying about my looks. I had a similar experience with clothing. For so long, no one had explained to me which fashions worked well on camera – or where I could find acceptable clothes for cheap. I didn't get any true advice until seven years into my career, when a fashion consultant came to my station in Atlanta and, in one hour, set me on the right path. Now I keep my eye on the latest trends and try to wear what makes me comfortable, but mostly I don't worry much about my clothes because I have learned the simple lessons of what works and what doesn't.

That is why this chapter is so important.

You do not want, as a solo video journalist, to work extraordinarily hard on your story and have it submarined by poor appearance. You also do not want to sacrifice your ability to shoot and tell an important story because you feel you must dress a certain way. Doing it all means solving the twin challenges of looking orderly on the air and being functional in the field. One must learn how to dress for both.

Heidi Wigdahl has her own embarrassing story about the balancing act of MMJ appearance.

It's the story of the poop shoes.

"Usually I wear a polo and jeans," says the soloist at KARE-TV in Minneapolis about her reporting outfit on the weekends. "That day, I just happened to wear a nice dress and some flats."

That day occurred five years into Wigdahl's career. She received an assignment ill-suited for flats on her feet: covering tornado cleanup efforts on a farm.

"The only way to get to all of the action was to go through the mud where the horses typically walk," Wigdahl recalls. "The mud and the poop were just kind of … they were basically mixed together into a whole slush."

The nearby farmers looked at Wigdahl with disbelief.

"They were all saying, 'No! No! You shouldn't go there!'" she says. "But I had to. Those were my visuals!"

Such is the MMJ life: sacrificing your comfort – and sometimes your shoes – for the story.

"I just tossed them," Wigdahl says of the fateful flats. "I mean, there was just no point in saving them. But on my way home, I got a flat tire and I still had those poop shoes on!"

Rarely does Wigdahl (Figure 2.2) get caught so, pardon the pun, flat-footed. She has risen quickly from a small market (Rochester, Minn.) to a medium-sized market (Knoxville, Tenn.) to, now, a large market and one of the top storytelling stations in the country. She has won several Regional Edward R. Murrow Awards and received the Upper Midwest Emmy for Video Journalist. She learned long ago she would need to give up some of the glamour of TV reporting to produce high-quality packages as a solo act.

Wigdahl did not mind. At her first job, she needed convincing to even consider her on-air appearance. An old mentor, longtime Chicago journalist Carol Marin, set her straight.

"I mentioned to Carol that I just don't have time to put on my make-up," Wigdahl recalls. "She got really serious with me and said, 'You have to make time. It's part of your job.' Her big thing was, 'When you go on the air, people cannot be distracted by how you look. If you go on with no make-up, people

Figure 2.2 Heidi Wigdahl.
Courtesy of David Peterlinz

are going to recognize that something's a little off. And it will distract from
your story.'

"I had never really looked at it that way – that it's part of being a journalist."

That idea, for so many, is a fundamental roadblock.

"It can be really demeaning, as a journalist, to have so much of your
appearance get picked apart," she told me. "You work for so long on a sweeps
piece, and you put your heart into the story, and then the one e-mail you get
is about the necklace you're wearing that the person didn't like."

Is one's appearance "part of being a journalist?"

Whether yes or no, it matters … for all the reasons Wigdahl learned
long ago.

Of course, that does not make life as a solo video journalist any simpler.

"That's always the challenge," Wigdahl says: "having to look like a reporter
while having the convenience of a photographer."

But one need not spend much time learning how to do it right.

Dressing for the Job

As you read this chapter, you will probably notice a common thread: women
get many more paragraphs than men.

That is because, regarding fashion, men typically have far fewer options.

"I actually think it's more challenging for men," Wigdahl says, "because men have a strict uniform."

Men on the air typically wear a shirt, tie, and blazer – and some form of dressy pants, in case the camera shoots wide. The problem? Those items can all be relatively expensive, especially for a journalist at his first job.

I struggled for a long time to find clothes that looked acceptable on the air but didn't cost too much. I did not want to hold back as a shooter to keep my shirts in pristine condition. If I stained one or ripped a seam, I wanted to be able to toss it just like Wigdahl tossed her $20 flats.

Then I discovered two secret weapons: discount department stores and clearance sales. TJ Maxx, Marshall's, and similar stores offer a tremendous variety of dress shirts for far cheaper than major department stores. If you like bigger names, you can benefit greatly from clearance sales. I regularly find great shirts at Macy's for less than $25 – all because they are on the clearance rack – and I keep an eye on online retailers.

In addition, I recommend wearing what I call the "fashion mullet" (Figure 2.3). Up top? Dressy for air. Below the belt? Less formal but more functional for shooting. I typically wear fitted jeans or khaki pants; they fit the criteria of being durable yet professional. I match them with a sturdy pair of brown shoes that look formal on camera but remain comfortable for walking.

Figure 2.3 Behold the "fashion mullet."

Credit: Nicole Leffer

I keep a suit jacket or blazer in either my car or the newsroom to wear during live shots.

It's that simple.

For women, it's not … but it's not much more difficult. In fact, the basic concept remains the same: save your fancier clothes for after you shoot.

"Even when I'm dressed up," Wigdahl says, "I'm wearing clothes that are easy to move around in."

This often means ditching the high heels and dresses for flat boots and blouses. Wigdahl does not particularly like blazers – "I'm much more suited to blouses and not structured clothing." But she keeps one at her desk for the same reason men keep suit jackets at theirs: "It makes you look instantly polished. I just put the blazer on, and automatically I look great on the air."

Regarding shoes, Wigdahl says she notices how young MMJs try to wear high heels in the field … and then quickly change their ways.

"I see them in the beginning wearing their heels, walking around, and going to stories," she says, "and then probably around three months in, it's like the heels are gone."

Why?

"I think they discover it's painful walking around in heels all day! You're lugging around a camera and a tripod, trying to get all of your interviews, doing all of these creative shots. This job is already so stressful and has so many demands. Your clothes should be the last thing that's a hurdle."

But you can still keep dressier items nearby for when you go on the air. High heels are one example. Necklaces are another.

"I really won't wear [a necklace] during the day," Wigdahl says: "because it just gets in the way. Then, when I put my make-up on, I put on the necklace to wear it on the air. I like it because it's a cheaper way to look like you have a more extravagant wardrobe. And if you're someone who likes to wear a blazer, but you only have a few, you can keep wearing statement necklaces, and they will make the outfit look totally different."

When Wigdahl goes to buy these items, she actually selects many of the same stores I recommended for the men – with a few additions. In addition to TJ Maxx, Marshall's, and Macy's, Wigdahl suggests shops like Ann Taylor Loft, Limited, and Forever 21.

The overall message? You need to dress nicely, but you must seek function in addition to form.

"I don't think anyone sees me come into an interview not wearing heels and says, 'Oh, you don't look like a reporter,'" she says. "I'm still able to look presentable, but obviously being comfortable is Number One. And most people understand that when they see you carrying all that equipment."

Wearing Hair and Make-Up

They will likely also understand if your hair and make-up are not in immaculate condition.

Again, for men, these subjects require far fewer pages. Because men typically wear shorter hair styles than women, they do not need to worry as much about upkeep in the field. They simply need to make sure their haircut is clean and does not blow around in the wind. Remember: at the end of the day, you may need to do a live shot outdoors. Powerful gusts of wind can turn even short hair into a mess. I personally use a matte gel, but many men reach for spray to keep their hair sturdy.

In terms of make-up, I only require two items: foundation and blot powder. The former gives my skin a smooth tone, and the latter prevents it from shining. I sweat quite a bit during the day, even if I don't notice at the time. That sweat develops into a film on my face; if I do not apply blot powder, I will look like an oily mess.

As for which brand, I was told long ago that MAC is "the industry standard." My experience with their products has confirmed that reputation.

For women, as usual, the matter gets slightly more complex. I have not been able to find a consensus on which brands and products make the most sense. Wigdahl offers one relatively universal truth: do not expect your 9 AM make-up to last through your 5 PM live shot.

"When I go into work," she says, "I am wearing all of my make-up, but by the time I go on the air, it will pretty much all be gone. Anything with the face – concealer, foundation, blush – will all be wiped away."

Wigdahl devotes ten minutes before each live shot to re-apply; she even carries a rollable make-up bag that she can hang from any bathroom stall – or, in some cases, a live truck door handle (see Figure 2.4).

When she feels particularly pressed, she focuses on one goal: "putting some color in my face to make sure I'm not washed out."

She recalls covering a protest in Minneapolis and being unable to break away to edit her story until hours after she had intended.

"I was editing the package until 4:40," Wigdahl recalls, "and I quickly had to put on some make-up. In that situation, where I didn't have much time to make myself presentable, I put on some blush and lipstick, and even though I wasn't wearing a lot of make-up in that live shot, I still looked OK."

Figure 2.4 Meet the world's most high-tech and expensive make-up bag hanger.

Credit: Heidi Wigdahl

The message? No matter how much time you spend before your day, reserve time before any on-air appearance to check your make-up. This counts for stand-ups, as well. Many female MMJs will carry a tiny make-up bag with the rest of their gear to any shoot. They will then be prepared to look presentable if they need to record a stand-up.

They will also, during that pre-air window, check and spray their hair.

Women's hair could probably take up its own chapter, and I do not profess to be an expert. But in talking with female solo video journalists, I have come away with a common theme; one articulated beautifully by Wigdahl:

"You just have to know your hair."

Specifically, you have to know how to wear your hair to require, for any time or situation, the lowest maintenance. Some MMJs, Wigdahl says, can "come in wearing perfect curls that stay all day." Others, like Wigdahl, cannot expect curls to hold over a grueling eight-hour span. A co-worker in Atlanta told me a few drops of rain or sweat can mean disaster for her hair, so, on a rainy or even humid day, she wraps a shawl around her head and neck.

Much like their male colleagues, many women also keep a giant bottle of hair spray at their desks and in their news vehicles.

Regardless of gender, a solo video journalist should approach hair and make-up with a mindset geared towards convenience. When your day ends, few people will see your presentable-but-not-perfect appearance during your shoots. Your whole audience, though, will see your appearance during your stand-ups and live shots. You should therefore focus your efforts towards those moments that will truly matter, directing your attention otherwise to your story.

Developing a Wardrobe

Of course, so much of the advice in this chapter comes down to an extension of a theme of Chapter 1: Know yourself.

Know what you like to wear. Know what clothing enables you to do your best work. Know the many ways in which your particular appearance is unique.

Once you know these things, you can be ready for whatever the day brings.

"You have to be prepared for anything," says Wigdahl. "You never know, at the beginning of the day, where you are going to end up. You just never know where you are going to be sent or what is going to happen."

Most MMJs – heck, most reporters – keep an emergency kit in the car. I rarely leave the station without taking a suit jacket with me. I set it in the back seat with a rain jacket and station cap. During the winter, I add to that list a sweater, gloves, and scarf.

(I used to keep snow boots as well, but they have not yet come in handy in Georgia.)

As for Wigdahl? "I always carry around jeans, a KARE11 shirt, and some rain boots," she says, along with snow boots for the winter. But she also includes a kit of select supplies for her appearance, many attuned to her individual needs:

- "I always keep my hair spray and a comb, because you never know if you are going to be able to come back to the station."
- "I carry around a lint brush roller. I have two cats, so I have cat hair on everything."
- "I like to have glasses with me just in case something happens to my contact lenses. I have this thing where one of my contacts starts acting up, and then it gets really bad and I can't read the teleprompter."

If you pay attention for a few weeks to your own routine, you will likely determine how to fill your emergency kit. Similar attention can guide you with your wardrobe.

"I was wearing this red dress on the air," Wigdahl told me, "and right after that, two anchors told me, 'Oh my gosh, you look so good in red.' And I just made a mental note of that."

Wigdahl recommends taking those comments to heart – to a point. I agree. You do not want to allow the words of others to affect you negatively, but you should be open to feedback.

This, of course, applies to everything as a journalist. I regularly seek critiques about my shooting, writing, editing, and overall effort. But I also look for advice about my appearance, even if that advice is not always kind. I know little about fashion, and I happily accept others' suggestions if I think they will benefit my work. At the same time, I try to keep from letting outside opinions drag me down.

Perhaps the best advice for anyone in this area is as follows: figure out the clothes and appearance in which you feel confident, and move forward with that confidence so you can focus on telling stories.

"I see how frequently people love to comment on everything people wear on the air," Wigdahl says: "I used to wear this one shade of red lipstick, and one time, at a city council meeting, this random guy just came straight up to me and said, 'You need to stop wearing that red lipstick on the air.' People think, because they see you on TV, they know you and can comment on things that are super-personal."

These matters are super-personal, but for anyone who appears on television, they are also super-public. Wigdahl boils down her philosophy to one sentence that addresses both:

"If you like something, and it's not distracting on air, you should wear it."

Sounds good to me.

Gearing Up 3

Figure 3.1

Credit: Matt Pearl

I have already mentioned the "five stages of shame."

I recounted, during Chapter 1, how I once left for a shoot without a tape on which to record – and how I have never made that mistake since. I discussed the importance, for all photographers but particularly solo video journalists, of developing a system for one's gear. Doing so simplifies the job and eliminates variables in what can often be an unpredictable environment.

But developing a system goes far beyond remembering a memory card and batteries.

It involves knowing and mastering all the equipment required to tell a great story – and enabling that equipment to help one's work, not hinder it.

The great Ira Glass of NPR once made a statement about creativity that seems to ripple regularly through my Facebook feed.

"All of us who do creative work," he said, "get into it because we have good taste. But it's like there's a gap. For the first couple of years you're making stuff, what you're making isn't so good … We [know] our work [doesn't] have this special thing we want it to have … It's gonna take you a while. It's normal to take a while, and you just have to fight your way through that." (PRI Public Radio International, 2009).

Many MMJs begin to win that fight when they truly understand the power of their tools. This can seem like an arduous process, and those who do not particularly enjoy photography might feel hesitant to invest in it. But if you want to produce high-quality work, you cannot avoid it.

I point to this quote from another esteemed journalist: "Know your gear. Know every single inch of it so when you're out on a story, you're reacting to what's happening around you, not what's happening with your gear. It seems silly that something we work with every single day could get in our way."

The man who said that has, throughout his career, raised the standard for solo video journalism.

I had never met Greg Bledsoe until I interviewed him for this book.

But I had admired his work for years, and I still do. The longtime MMJ for KNSD-TV in San Diego has twice been named the National Press Photographers Association's Solo Video Journalist of the Year.

"I remember telling my wife the first night that I won it," Bledsoe told me over lunch. "I get chills thinking about it."

He won the crown for 2011 and 2012 for consistently producing one-man masterpieces that outshone competition from across the country – myself included.

The NPPA would, after every competition, post videos of the award-winning stories. I regularly marveled at Bledsoe's. At the time I often felt frantic in the field, trying in vain to capture moments and somehow make sense of unpredictable environments. When I watched Bledsoe's stories, I felt he showed extraordinary command. He developed rich characters and made

Figure 3.2 Greg Bledsoe.

Credit: Matt Pearl

me care about them. He composed frame-worthy shots even during chaos. He never seemed in a rush, eternally confident in the power of his material.

He continues that command today. Bledsoe (Figure 3.2) took a writing job with KNSD in 2001 and has worked at the station ever since – first writing, then producing, then field producing, then tracking packages and doing live shots, and eventually becoming one of the country's finest MMJs. These days he co-anchors the station's morning and midday shows but still carves out time to produce long-form features.

Upon meeting him, I learned he often feels as frantic as the rest of us.

"You can never orchestrate the best story," Bledsoe told me. "You never plan the best moments. You're just running around, and then they happen."

With Bledsoe, they seem to happen more often, in part because he possesses a tremendous understanding of his gear. When we met, he showed me his work vehicle and system for organizing equipment. We also swapped tips and techniques that serve as a great foundation for utilizing that equipment.

This chapter discusses that foundation – a critical and conquerable step in one's development as a soloist.

"We know how hard it really is," Bledsoe says of working as a one-person operation. "But we shouldn't be held to any different bar because we do it on our own."

Indeed, solo video journalists should aim to reach the same bar as everyone else … and then clear it.

Organizing Your Gear

That starts with developing a system for your equipment and figuring out how to store and transport it in your news vehicle.

Most MMJs design their systems around two three-word sentences:

Keep it safe. Keep it simple.

"I think gear is fun and can definitely make stories look better," says Bledsoe, who owns a DSLR camera but only occasionally uses it for his job. "The reality is, most of us can't afford the best toys, and you really don't need them to tell a great story."

Instead, figure out what toys you do need. Then determine the safest and simplest way to carry them. Your most important piece of equipment, of course, is the camera. Many news vans are equipped with designated units or lock boxes to keep cameras secure. Others offer no such protection, but photographers can use their camera bags or other means to provide the necessary padding. Bledsoe leaves his camera loose but surrounds it with several bags that are filled with packaging, leaving little risk of it moving around or tipping over (see Figure 3.3). I use a similar strategy for my tripod, nestling it in the trunk next to the backpack that stores my lights.

Speaking of lights, they present a unique transportation challenge. A light kit consists of numerous items: stands, plugs (unless the lights are battery powered), filters or gels, and the bulbs or panels themselves. Many MMJs

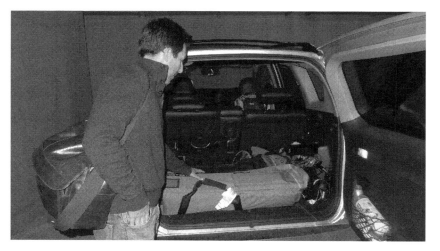

Figure 3.3 Bledsoe uses every inch of trunk space to arrange his equipment.

Credit: Matt Pearl

steer away from the hurdle of organizing that gear, mainly because they lack familiarity and don't want to invest the time to learn and understand it.

Here is where a backpack becomes a terrific tool.

I carry, in a standard two-shoulder strap pack, everything necessary to light an interview. I remove all frills and fill the bag with what I need: everything listed above, minus the gels, plus headphones. (Before I switched to dimmable lights, I also carried a diffusion umbrella that slid neatly next to my light stands.) When I arrive at an indoor shoot, I can simply sling the pack over my shoulders and keep both hands free to carry my camera and tripod.

Bledsoe maintains his kit with a similar mindset: "I keep two very simple, battery-powered lights. I think, a lot of times, people don't light stuff because they think it's a hassle. But this stuff," he says, pointing to his pack, "is so easy that I don't have to think twice."

I would recommend two other bags:

- The must-have: This is a smaller bag that holds microphones, batteries, and memory cards – mainly to avoid the aforementioned five stages of shame.
- The computer bag: One-person crews often receive their own laptops, which turn into mobile edit bays and require cases to support that. I use mine to store miscellaneous items: my IFB (interruptible foldback), make-up, an extra set of headphones, and obviously my laptop and accessories.

(Bledsoe also carries a duffel bag with a change of clothes, following the advice in Chapter 2 about always keeping a spare wardrobe in your car.)

If you receive your own car, you can generally rest easy, loading and maintaining it as you wish. But many are not so lucky. They share with their coworkers a car and, in some cases, a camera.

"Sharing gear is tough," Bledsoe says. "When you're working out of a different car every day, you really do need to be pretty compact and even more simplified."

You also need to stick to your system and design it for portability. I, for example, do not share a news vehicle, so I can soup mine up (very modestly) with a USB cord, bottles of water, hand sanitizer, and a suit jacket. I do not need to worry about removing and resetting these items every day. At my first job, I shared a vehicle, so I stored miscellaneous items in a plastic bag at my cubicle and transported them back and forth. I basically created another storage case for myself and saved time I would have spent searching when I needed to leave for a shoot.

Carrying Your Gear

When you arrive at a shoot, you want to run with a similar philosophy: carry your gear so you don't have to worry about it.

"I want as little gear as I can when I'm out shooting something," says Bledsoe, "because unless you are sitting in someone's house where you have the luxury of stashing all of your gear in the corner, you are normally at scenes where you have to move around a lot. I don't want to leave a bag in a public place and have to keep looking over my shoulder to make sure it's there."

What should you do instead? When in doubt, take only what fits in your hands and pockets.

"For the most part," says Bledsoe, "with my camera in one hand and my tripod in the other, I can shoot 95% of daily news."

It's true. You should certainly learn and appreciate the extra toys and add-ons, but for most stories, you will not need them. In many cases, you will not want them. You will want to focus simply on capturing great sound bites and moments, not tracking every piece of equipment in your arsenal.

Bledsoe once found himself on a shoot where he actively avoided carrying anything but the essentials.

"There was a guy who was an injured vet," he recalls, "who lost both of his legs to an IED in Iraq."

That guy? Marine Staff Sergeant Mark Zambron. The double amputee was preparing to climb Mount Kilimanjaro. "One of his training hikes was at a place called Mt. Woodson here in San Diego. So I show up, and I have my tripod and camera, and we do a six-mile hike – me with my full gear."

That hike, by the way, features an elevation gain of 2,000 feet. It typically takes three hours to complete.

"What, was I going to complain?" laughs Bledsoe. "This guy was climbing it while missing both legs!"

Bledsoe climbed it too, shooting a beautiful story that captured first place in that quarter's NPPA competition. A viewer would never guess the physical strain behind it – or the minimal equipment.

Of course, few stories require a six-mile hike. But each story brings its own conditions and circumstances, which require a one-person crew to assess each shoot individually before deciding which gear to bring. For example:

- Will the weather be a factor? Pack your rain gear – or, if necessary, a garbage bag – to protect your camera from getting wet.

- Are you shooting an interview indoors? Bring the backpack with your light kit, because you will not need to worry about keeping track of it.
- Will you be away from your vehicle for a while? Take a spare battery so you don't get caught without one.

It all comes down to knowing your gear and picking your spots.

As Bledsoe says, people "who do what you and I do, we have only two hands, not four."

But those two hands can produce great work … if the person attached to them understands his or her tools.

Learning the Camera

I will spend the next three chapters examining the process of shooting a story. I will provide my philosophy for capturing high-quality video and audio, and I will share tips and techniques that most effectively promote that philosophy.

But none of it will matter if I do not first address the basics: the three settings that a wise photographer learns almost immediately after picking up a camera.

The overarching theme can be summed up in two words: no AUTO.

"You never want your settings on AUTO," says Bledsoe: "[If you do] you will have settings changing during the middle of a shot. The camera detects a shift in light, and all of a sudden it does things you didn't ask it to do, right at the moment when a person says something great."

The faster you learn about a camera's most fundamental controls – focus, zoom, and the iris – the faster you will develop as a shooter.

Focus, of course, is essentially another word for visual clarity or sharpness. Most newcomers understand the concept from their own experiences with still photography. We can all identify – and have probably taken – pictures that seem either beautifully crisp or unintentionally blurry.

The process becomes slightly more complex when shooting video.

A typical camera includes a wheel on the lens to control a shot's focal length. It also features a viewfinder or LCD screen to check one's work in real time. The viewfinder, though, because of its tiny size, does not always provide the most precise snapshot.

As a result, many MMJs – Bledsoe and me included – take an extra step before pressing RECORD to ensure the sharpest image.

"You zoom all the way in," Bledsoe says, on whatever you want to shoot, "set your focus, and then zoom all the way back."

The zoom, in this case, works like a magnifying glass, providing a photographer with an extreme close-up of his or her subject. Some cameras offer an artificial focus expander – a button that digitally zooms even further to create a similar effect.

You can use these options to set your focus in seconds.

The zoom, at its simplest, does just what its name suggests: it enables the camera operator to frame a shot as wide or tight as desired. It also allows her or him to capture detailed shots while staying in the background.

"You like to make people more comfortable by not sticking a camera in their faces," Bledsoe says. "We are, in effect, silent observers of what we're recording, and it's easier to be that silent observer if you're not two feet away."

Most newcomers understand the basic features of the zoom function. Few realize its effect on a shot's depth of field, which refers to the distance between the nearest and farthest objects in a scene that appear in focus. Zooming in actually reduces this depth, creating a seemingly sharper subject with a blurrier background. Zooming out produces the opposite effect, allowing the entire scene to appear in focus.

A photographer can also control the depth of field – and several other factors – by opening and closing the camera's iris.

The iris, or aperture, dictates how much light enters the camera. Open it up, and your shot will get brighter. Of course, if you fail to open the iris enough, your shot will look too dark. If you open it too much, your shot will look overexposed.

You must thus seek the right balance every time. You can do this by checking your camera's viewfinder or LCD screen – or by utilizing zebra stripes, which show up on the screen wherever your shot is overexposed. The "zebras" come as an option on most modern video cameras. I never use them, but Bledsoe relies on them.

"It gives me a cue of something that's always the same," he says. "It's a consistency from story to story where I see it and I'm like, 'OK. I know where I am.'"

The iris also helps to determine a shot's depth of field. A nearly closed iris will produce a wide depth of field where the whole scene looks sharp (see Figure 3.4). A fully open iris will cause the opposite, blurring everything but a shot's focal point (see Figure 3.5). Most photographers aim to keep their fields shallow, particularly when shooting interviews.

Figures 3.4 Wide depth of field.

Credit: Matt Pearl

Figures 3.5 Shallow depth of field.

Credit: Matt Pearl

"If I'm doing an interview with someone, I want to knock out as much background as possible," Bledsoe says. "I love to have the iris open as much as I can, because I love that soft background. And we don't get that a whole lot with video cameras."

You can learn quite a bit from playing with the three basic components: focus, zoom, and the iris. But you should also aim to master a secondary but similarly critical trio of settings:

- White balance: The camera uses this function to perfectly replicate a scene's colors. A photographer typically sets it whenever entering a new environment. He or she simply zooms in on a white object and presses the "white balance" button. The camera does the rest.
- Shutter speed: This measures how much time is required to capture a frame of video. A quicker shutter speed (typically less than 1/60th of a second) produces a crisper image.
- Macro: This option, as Bledsoe says, "gives you the best depth of field and perspectives you can't get from a regular camera." It typically provides increased sharpness and detail on close-up shots. It also reduces the depth of field.

"A lot of these things seem basic, but they're really simple and really effective," says Bledsoe, referring specifically to the beginner techniques that can quickly become instinctive. "They are things you and I make sure we do every time, and that happens by getting into good habits from the very beginning."

That sums up the basic mantra of this chapter: develop a foundation as early as you can, and enable yourself to focus on what matters: the stories you produce.

Reference

PRI Public Radio International (2009, August 18). "Ira Glass on Storytelling, Part 3 of 4" [video file]. Retrieved from www.youtube.com/watch?v=BI23U7U2aUY&feature=channel)

Thinking Digital

4

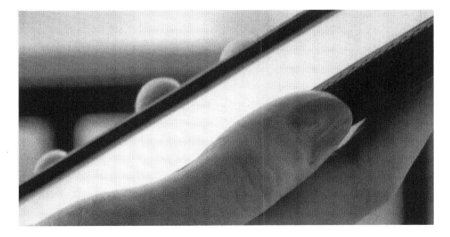

Figure 4.1

Credit: Matt Pearl

Recently my family and I moved into our first house, which meant caring for our first lawn. I had never tended to an outdoor space larger than a balcony, and the yard I inherited with my house was patchy and unkempt. So I did my research. I read gardening blogs, scanned the big-bag aisles at Home Depot, and quickly turned into "that guy" who's really into his lawn. *You want to talk mulch? What fertilizer do you use? Is that Kentucky bluegrass or zoysia?*

It didn't work.

Every week I'd mow my lawn, step back onto the driveway, survey my progress, and wonder why I wasn't seeing results. I'd look at my neighbors' pristine, finely manicured gardens and ask myself, "What am I doing wrong? Why doesn't mine look like theirs?"

Sometimes, as a journalist, I feel the same way about social media.

I follow best practices, post at specific times, spread my stories on multiple platforms, and stay as consistent as I can despite a chaotic schedule. I often see results. But seemingly just as often, I don't. I look at the statistics, and I can't ignore or spin them in my head. Digital success is a question of numbers: likes, shares, comments, retweets, reposts, new follows. We all know when we don't have them.

Like it or not, digital success is part of how many journalists get judged. Stations keep social media scoreboards, pitting reporters against each other. They intertwine on-air with online and expect their storytellers to shine on both. Yes, television still keeps the lights on, but the digital shine is growing fast as generations change and viewing habits shift. Its importance even shows in this book. In the first version of *The Solo Video Journalist*, I wrote a chapter called "Working the Web" and placed it towards the back, after the chapters that focused on storytelling for broadcast. This time, this chapter is near the front, and its content has evolved. In so many ways, digital now comes first – for all journalists, solo or otherwise.

Incoming MMJs aren't surprised by this.

If you enter adulthood in the 2020s, you were barely a baby when Facebook gained its first users. You were in elementary school, maybe, when Twitter took off. You were in middle school or junior high when Instagram became more than just a library of your friends' photos. And you were in or near high school when NBC launched a newscast built for Snapchat.

New MMJs don't need to be convinced of the permanence of social media – or its importance to their careers. You want to know how to use it right. You want to learn how to feed multiple digital platforms while producing stories for multiple newscasts. You want to post not just frequently but effectively. You don't want to waste your time. You want to shine.

This chapter, then, serves two purposes. First, it provides tools and tactics for building a steady digital presence during your already overloaded workday. Second, it offers advice on how to go beyond treading water and develop a brand that prioritizes your online identity.

It's fueled by two social media standouts who helped me get my digital lawn in order … and who approach the subject with seemingly opposite mindsets.

⌒♫⌒

Tiffany Liou and Neima Abdulahi know what it means to juggle multiple jobs.

Less than a year after graduating with a business degree and landing a marketing job, Liou (Figure 4.2) realized she couldn't shake her itch for news. She snagged an internship at KTVU, the FOX affiliate in the Bay Area, and eventually earned a paying position as an overnight assignment editor. But she never quit her day job. She worked 9-to-5 at Salesforce, and several nights a week she crossed the bay to Oakland to monitor scanners from midnight to 8 AM.

Some days, Liou says, "I slept in a Target parking lot in Hayward" – halfway between the two offices – "because I was so tired I couldn't get home."

The double duty paid off. Within a year, she was offered an MMJ position in West Monroe, Louisiana and drove 2,000 miles east to begin her career in journalism. "I saw the difference it could make," she recalls. "I saw the people it could help. News can be depressing, but it can also bring out the good in people ... and the hope."

Abdulahi (Figure 4.3) didn't face such a stark choice. She's just couldn't choose between her passions.

"I thought I wanted to be a rapper," she laughs. "But in high school I realized I didn't want to be broke with a dream."

Instead, she devoured news, working on Decatur High School's monthly 15-minute newscast that would air during homeroom. She told stories

Figure 4.2 Tiffany Liou.
Courtesy of Tiffany Liou

Figure 4.3 Neima Abdulahi.

Credit: Matt Pearl

of classmates whose communities hadn't always received a schoolwide megaphone. She studied broadcast journalism at Elon University and interned at the FOX station in Atlanta. But she never closed the door on music. She juggled her TV internship with a program assistant position across town at the city's premier hip-hop radio station, V-103.

"I would do eight hours at a news station and then six hours after with the radio," she recalls. "So I've always been a hustler, doing lots of things."

Today, Liou is an Emmy-winning MMJ for one of the premier storytelling shops in the country, WFAA in Dallas. Abdulahi produced long-form reports about the Atlanta music scene while turning daily stories solo for her hometown's NBC affiliate, WXIA, before leaving the station at the end of 2019.

Both thrive on social media.

Liou has amassed thousands of followers on Facebook and Twitter, where she receives regular engagement and reaction to meaningful stories. Abdulahi has built a dominant presence across platforms but particularly on Instagram, with tens of thousands of followers and an online brand almost entirely divorced from her work for TV.

Together, they provide fascinating case studies – and paths for solo video journalists who seek guidance on the digital landscape.

Understanding the Platforms

In some ways, this chapter is a challenge. Social media platforms evolve quickly. They fade in and out of favor. New apps emerge, and one-time new apps disappear. How does one offer advice that won't expire with the next adjustment of an algorithm?

But within the chaos stands general consistency. For the past decade, the digital landscape has remained remarkably stable – at least in how it affects journalists. In particular, the Big Three – Facebook, Twitter, and Instagram – have developed their own identities that can be utilized in different ways.

Facebook remains the dominant platform. It also remains the biggest driver of traffic away from the platform. Despite a recent algorithm change that deprioritized publishers, Facebook continues to be the most direct way, by far, to promote and push viewers to your stories. It's also a free-for-all, where posts from the last three hours jockey with those from the last three days.

Twitter, on the other hand, tends to reward what's new. Most TV reporters prefer it for breaking news and press conferences, where they can provide unrelenting updates and not be penalized. In these cases, Liou says, "it's my best friend."

Instagram offers a canvas to define your brand beyond your work. It remains the least friendly as far as embedding links and funneling viewers to your full-length reports. It also doesn't prioritize or display news with the same prominence as its fellow social media titans. But it emphasizes visuals, with each post requiring a photo or video, and tends to attract a younger audience. "Instagram," says Abdulahi, "is the conversation."

These three platforms have endured and evolved for journalistic use in ways others haven't. They offer ample opportunities to promote your work and showcase your energy. It all sounds great, except for two overarching questions that loom over MMJs everywhere:

One: How are you going to fill all this space?

Two, and more importantly: Who's got the time to figure it out?

Turns out we all do. We just need to be strategic.

In Chapter 1 I talked about time management and planning your day in advance. Many solo video journalists approach their digital responsibilities the same way. They scan their schedule for pockets of time that often go unused – or, at least, where they feel they can spare a few minutes to ensure they find time for digital.

I scatter mine throughout the day:

- I take 10–15 minutes when I first arrive
- I take 2–3 minutes in my car after each shoot
- I take 10 minutes at lunch
- I take 2–3 minutes after I return while loading raw footage onto my laptop.

Typically that provides enough windows to put out several well-formulated posts. Liou works dayside as well, so she adjusts her workflow around her story. "When I'm out," she says, "I try to at least take a photo on my phone" and get it to Facebook. If she's at a press conference or trial, she'll lean on Twitter and live-tweet as much as she can. Abdulahi worked the morning shift, which typically began with a two-hour block on-air where she worked with a photographer. That's when she grazed on Twitter. She would send a half-dozen tweets between live shots, often about her own developing story.

And our stories are our best sources for content. We can strip them to the marrow to amplify them online.

Telling Your Story ... Digitally

The digital world offers unlimited space. In many ways, that's daunting. But it's also an opportunity for reporters to expand stories beyond 90 seconds in a newscast. They can turn their assignments into a dozen posts online without adding too much effort.

The easiest way? Take photos.

Particularly for Facebook and Instagram, you'll need them.

You can, of course, use your phone to snap a few shots while you're on your shoot. But you can also scan your raw footage when you return and use your editing software to capture still images of the strongest frames. If you want, you can use the software's title tool or a photo / text app for your phone (a quick Google search should show the latest and best) to add a particularly powerful quote from one of your interviews. As an MMJ, you control your story's visual look, and you use professional-grade gear to do it. Lean into that advantage, and find those frames that couldn't possibly have been shot with an iPhone.

Of course, your greatest advantage is your access to video: clean, sharp, high-quality video that can stop someone's Newsfeed scroll in its tracks. If I know I have shot a meaningful moment, I upload the raw clip to Facebook or Twitter almost instantly upon returning. Sometimes I snip a sound bite – the kind of bite I'd plaster as a quote on a photo – and post it unedited. When I have time, I produce 30-second teases from my footage, add a music bed and border, and give my features an unmistakable visual look.

On the rare occasion, I simply post a segment of my on-air package, such as in the fall of 2018, when one walk down an aisle reached tens of thousands overnight.

Ally Poole could see her life coming together. She aspired to be a nurse, and she had just begun a rapidly blooming romance with a young man named Amos. The two had even picked out a puppy and named her Lily. One day, while driving Lily to the vet, Ally saw a hay truck swerve into her lane on a winding road. Her car flipped. She was thrown yards away. When she awoke weeks later at the hospital, she couldn't feel her legs. Her spine was shattered.

Amos stuck by her. Ally pushed forward. She rehabbed and worked to rebuild strength in her legs. Nearly five years later, the couple got married, and Ally – with her father holding her on one side and her stepfather on the other – walked 50 feet into her soon-to-be-husband's grasp.

I witnessed the moment in person. I produced a 3 ½-minute story and saved Ally's momentous steps for the end. Then I clipped the final minute of my package, including my voice track, and posted it to Facebook.

It didn't take long to take off.

Not only did Ally's walk reach 80,000 people online, it held their attention. A larger-than-usual percentage watched the whole clip, and thousands responded with likes, loves, comments, and shares. I received tens of thousands of eyeballs from viewers who wouldn't have otherwise seen my work.

So much of social media success comes down to content. To put it plainly, are you telling your viewers something they didn't know? Are you showing them something they'll want to spread? Sometimes, as with Ally's walk, it's as clear as Maldives water. Sometimes, particularly if you're on a story already receiving major coverage, you need to find a unique angle.

That's how Abdulahi produced one of her most popular videos: a lyrical quiz about Outkast.

In late 2019, a muralist unveiled a 30-foot tribute to the legendary Atlanta hip-hop duo. That day, everyone from the AJC to CNN shared the news. Abdulahi – who produced a weekly ATL Culture segment that seemed the perfect vehicle for the story – wanted to join the fray.

But she held back – at least, for a day.

Not wanting to compete with the immediate scrum of similar-sounding posts, Abdulahi says, "I asked myself, 'What's the Day Two coverage?' So I went out and quizzed fans" – many of whom had flocked to the mural to pose for photos – "about Outkast lyrics. I came up with questions no one would know about Outkast except those who really followed them."

She turned the story for air that Friday. A day later she trimmed it to 60 seconds and posted it to Instagram, where it received so many views that Big Boi himself reposted it – and followed her page.

"Social media can take two different routes," Abdulahi said in retrospect. "You're either part of the conversation or you're creating it."

Abdulahi's example enforces an important point: not every story demands immediacy. Not every story demands a half-dozen posts before you've even figured it out.

"Sometimes we don't have time," Liou says. "There are definitely days when I think, 'This can wait until 6 o'clock to post.' My old station asked us to post 3–5 times a day on Facebook and multiple times on Twitter. That was asking a lot. There were some days where I didn't accomplish that."

It's more important, she says, to be consistent, even if not always as frequently. Abdulahi agrees. When she covered breaking news, she often didn't post her stories on Facebook and Instagram, because – unlike Twitter – those platforms didn't necessarily reward posts with short shelf lives.

There's another, perhaps more obvious reason.

"If I don't make air," Liou points out, "that's not good. I need my job."

Indeed, most of us still get paid primarily for turning a product for television. Even at stations that claim to be digital-first, the deadlines of digital are far more fluid than the 90-second windows of a scheduled newscast. If your story doesn't make slot? "You're in somebody's room getting yelled at," laughs Abdulahi.

"And I don't want to be in nobody's office."

Crafting Your Online Identity

At a base level, you can fill a quota and build a following by documenting your on-air work on various social platforms. But there's another dimension to digital success: where you carve an identity beyond – and sometimes separate from – the stories you produce for television.

This is where you build your brand.

This is also where many of us, myself included, often scoff.

I'm a journalist, not a marketer. And I want to tell other people's stories, not my own.

But in an era where sharp-eyed viewers critique a reporter's biography as much as his or her work, we can all appreciate the value of platforms that allow us to connect more directly with our viewers. We can also utilize those platforms to make a meaningful impact – and not just through our stories.

For inspiration, check out Abdulahi on Instagram. In a few years, she has cultivated a consistent and devoted following by curating content with the platform – and its audience – in mind.

"When I was growing up and watched the news," she recalls, "I saw a portrayal that wasn't always accurate about our communities. There was always something missing: relatability and intentionality." Social media, she says, "gives a voice to diverse communities in a way that traditional media doesn't. You get a raw, unapologetic version of how things are affecting people."

If the above paragraph describes Abdulahi's mission statement, her daily posts on Instagram display how she achieves it. She speaks of her ancestry in Somalia and her childhood in public housing in Atlanta. She raps along with the radio to her favorite ATL classics. And she always experiments. I remember when Abdulahi launched an online-only series called ATLingo. She recruited one of our newest investigative reporters for a segment where she explained a term that only Atlantans would understand. It was a hit, both inside and outside our newsroom, but it didn't last long. Abdulahi stuck with it for three episodes, and when it no longer served its purpose, she dropped it. We should always avoid standing still for too long – at our jobs, in our careers, and onward. Abdulahi makes it an ethos online.

She also doesn't hide her hustle. She operates her accounts like a social media marketer, and she wouldn't think to do otherwise. When she posts 16×9 videos on Instagram, she fills the bars above and beneath them with a title and her handle. That way, if the video gets reposted, anyone who sees it will know who made it.

"You have to make sure you're branding your content," she says, "so people can come back and follow you. You're creating a community, and that community looks to you to facilitate conversations."

Abdulahi tracks her posts like a market analyst watches the Dow. She figures out what receives the strongest responses and doubles down on the techniques that achieve them. When I interviewed her, she spoke about using red as a standout font, searching the metrics of hashtags, and posting early in the morning to get into people's Newsfeeds first. Will these tactics remain effective when you read this paragraph? Maybe. But will Abdulahi adjust if they don't? And will she still create images and videos that run first or only on digital? Absolutely.

For Liou, it's different. She doesn't work the morning shift like Abdulahi, so she doesn't receive as much downtime on the fringes of her day. She fits in posts rather than letting them dictate her schedule. But she still understands her online identity, and she connects with her audience in ways that are just as meaningful.

"I'm a general assignment reporter," Liou says, "so I don't know if I have one specific type of follower. But I will say that people follow me from my markets, and they continue after I leave. They say, 'We miss you in the Quad Cities!' or 'We miss you in Oklahoma City!'"

I can relate. My digital audience has built up through hundreds of human-interest stories, each of which brings its own wave of new followers. They don't all exist in one city or region, but they tend to appreciate the depth, positivity, and inspiration of my work. Same goes for Liou. So when she recognizes a story that taps into that depth, she goes deep in discussing it.

In 2018, for instance, she went to Haiti to mark the eighth anniversary of the magnitude-7 earthquake that killed hundreds of thousands and affected millions. "I found a local Oklahoma connection," Liou recalls, "and asked my boss if I could go." The morning of her departure, she posted a photo of herself at the Oklahoma City airport, passport and luggage in hand, and wrote about the trip to come. Hundreds liked it. Dozens commented. And they stayed engaged throughout.

"People were really interested in that journey," she said. "When I came back, people were like, 'Oh, you're the girl that went to Haiti!' And most of it was people following on social media."

These kinds of victories – for these kinds of stories – feel euphoric. That's because they don't always come so easily.

"It's a hate-love relationship," Liou says. "Sometimes I'm surprised by how many people respond. Sometimes I make a post and am like, 'Oh, this is going to do well!' … and it gets five likes, and they're from my best friends."

Most in the storytelling community can tell near-identical stories.

The landscape of social media is always changing, and it involves an uncomfortable amount of public failure. I used to describe my philosophy as that of a swing-for-the-fences baseball player who either hits home runs or strikes out – no singles, doubles, or anything in-between. I still feel that way to a point, and I try not to get too dismayed when I whiff. My new lawn at home finally blossomed after months of mulching, seeding, and fertilizing. I keep the same persistence with my garden of social media accounts.

"I'll never understand it," Liou admits, speaking for 90% of the MMJs out there. "I just try to keep moving with it."

Career Chronicles

The Atypical Lane

My love for the camera didn't arrive in a choir-filled epiphany. It chipped away between whistles, buzzers, and the screeches of high-tops against hard maple on high school basketball courts across Iowa.

I was 22 years old, nearly six months into my first job in television, when my station in Sioux City cut its budgets by firing all of its main anchors. I wasn't a main anchor. I was the weekend sports guy. That day, the first Monday of the new year, my news director brought me into his office, explained the situation, and told me I would – effective immediately – take over as sports director. And who would replace me? No one. I would direct a department of one. I would produce, shoot, write, edit, and anchor two sportscasts a night.

Because January was just five days old, that meant I would need to shoot a lot of high school basketball. For the next two months, I spent nearly every weeknight at gyms across the region – a spread-out region where each game seemed 30 minutes from the previous one. I would finish the early evening newscast at 6:30, swing through a nearby McDonald's or Wendy's, spend an hour or two on the road, and return by 9:15 so I could get on the air an hour later. This gave me ten minutes – at most 15 – at the games themselves to capture enough highlights and cutaways to produce a 30-second recap.

And I loved it.

I loved the challenge. I loved the spontaneity and speed of the games. I loved the focus required to track the ball and anticipate its path. I loved the thrill of following a play from start to end and framing it just right. I loved the adrenaline rush of getting back to the station, editing the highlights, timing them with my script, and calling the plays live on television – all in barely an hour.

By season's end, I had become infatuated with the camera, unwilling to let it go.

My journey has always avoided tradition, at least somewhat. I didn't start in news; I started in sports. I didn't produce two packages a day; I produced two sportscasts a night. I largely stayed away from the grind of small- and medium-market reporting, and by the time I arrived at my third job in Atlanta – a full-time position in news, not sports – I had already carved a niche as a feature storyteller who specialized in long-form assignments. I didn't mind covering news of the day, but I knew I didn't see it as my long-term path, and I worked to create a lane I found more fulfilling.

That lane – an enterprise segment that has taken me out of the mix entirely – remains rare in video journalism, particularly for those who work alone. But it's not as rare as it once was.

When I entered the business, a solo video journalist's career arc seemed preordained: start in a small market, rise to a medium and then large market, and turn daily news stories for the next 30 years – assuming local television news lasted that long. In the past decade, the options have multiplied. Local newsrooms elevate MMJs to enterprise positions and investigative units. Digital outlets peer into an unlimited landscape and need video journalists who can fill it. Startups and nonprofits offer opportunities for documentarians to rent gear and make their own films. Even the most traditional and prestigious news outlets have opened their doors and allowed soloists to lead – and, in the process, find careers that embrace and fulfill their camera-infatuated hopes.

This chapter focuses on those possibilities, through the eyes of two storytellers determined to shoot as long as they can.

Nearly 700 miles south of Sioux City, Sarah Blake Morgan also began to embrace the camera six months into her first job. But she didn't stumble her way into it. She made a choice.

"It was a happiness decision for me," Morgan says. "I was miserable, stressed, and completely overwhelmed."

Morgan (Figure CC1.1) was in Lubbock, a market that doesn't even crack the Top 10 in Texas. She didn't want to be there. She didn't want to be in the United States. She aspired to be a foreign correspondent, a dream that germinated in her teens and solidified in college where she visited Egypt and Israel and, she says, "cried when I left because I felt completely at home." Morgan aimed to report from the Middle East. She didn't think she could do so alone.

But, Morgan realized, she had spent too many days scraping together stories and complaining about them afterward. She decided she couldn't afford to stiff-arm the camera. Instead, she would master it.

Figure CC1.1 Sarah Blake Morgan.

Courtesy of Sarah Blake Morgan

"That simple flip of the switch," she says, "showed in my work almost immediately."

She has never flipped back … even now, at one of the largest news agencies in the world.

Morgan works as a video journalist for the Associated Press. She covers the Southeast region of the US and, when large enough news breaks, the rest of the country. Her work is scattered across the Internet and television stations worldwide, often in countries many time zones ahead. She is a long way from Lubbock but with two common threads: she shoots her own stories, and she works alone.

She's not the only one of her kind with the company.

"A massive amount of the AP's revenue comes from video and their video subscribers," Morgan says. The AP has hired video journalists for years, but the job title remains loosely defined. "We have VJs that shoot VOSOTs but don't do a lot of packages or produce print stories. But I do. I made very clear what I want."

That mindset seems to be the through-line of Morgan's career arc: recognize your ambitions and use your solo status to help achieve them. In her case, Morgan began pitching assignments in Lubbock that hemmed closer to her international aspirations. Less than a year after her "flip of the switch,"

Morgan convinced her bosses to send her solo to Haiti, where she embedded with a local nonprofit and produced a weeklong series about its work at an orphanage in Montrouis. Stations in Market #143 don't typically budget for international travel, but Morgan figured out a way in.

All the while, she embraced every part of her west Texas experience.

"I am the reporter I am because of Lubbock," she says. "In a big market, you don't get much of a learning curve. But I was able to cover big regional stories at 21 years old. I was like, 'Hey, let me do it! Let me do it!' And they let me do it."

After two years in Lubbock, Morgan arrived at WBTV in Charlotte, N.C. Again, she pitched beyond the budget. In late 2016 she angled to cover American Airlines' first Charlotte-based flight to Cuba – a trip that was temporarily shelved when, days before takeoff, former president Fidel Castro died. "My bosses were like, 'OK, Castro died, so we're just going to cancel the trip.' I was like, 'Yeah, Castro died. Can I still go?'"

She went.

For the most part, Morgan spent her time in Charlotte building her chops and covering major local and regional stories by herself. Eventually she reached a point familiar to many: she was ready to leave local news. "Most people don't see themselves as MMJs for life because it's a grueling existence in many newsrooms," she says. "Maybe it would be different if we didn't abuse our talent."

That drain of talent – a "mass exodus," Morgan calls it – is a sad reality of the industry. Many MMJs exit journalism entirely. Others seek rare and often tenuous prestige positions within local shops. Some, like Morgan, find power in alternative platforms, even when the alternative is a news agency with 3,200 employees.

With these alternative platforms, solo video journalists can often develop their own workflow. Except during breaking news, Morgan produces roughly one story a week, almost always from ideas she pitches and cultivates from her bureau. She still wants to get to the Middle East, and she has smartly positioned herself in places that bring her closer.

She keeps her camera tucked under her arm.

"I don't see myself ever giving up shooting," she says. "I see myself telling the stories of people affected by the conflict – the people we sometimes forget about. I just have this vision of me and a Syrian refugee and my camera. I don't see a whole crew. I don't see a whole production. It's just us.

"I'm a better journalist because I'm by myself."

⁊

Around the time Sarah Blake Morgan flipped the switch in Lubbock, Dougal Shaw began to realize his future in London.

Ten years earlier, he had received his PhD in Early Modern Cultural History from Peterhouse, Cambridge. Over the next decade, he ingrained himself with the BBC, first as a researcher and producer on a long-form interview show, then as a writer and editor for the on-demand video team. Now he planned to develop a new lane.

"As a producer," Shaw recalls, "you learned to work with camera crews. It was the same with editing. You weren't allowed to edit by yourself, so I'd sit with an editor and say, 'Can you do this? Can you do that? Can you do this again?' I found that very frustrating, because I was quite a creative person, and I wanted to do all this stuff myself."

Now he does.

Shaw (Figure CC1.2) fills many roles at the BBC, but they all involve him producing features for its web site and TV stations, and they all involve him working alone. He handles segments named Future Designs, Weird Workplaces, and CEO Secrets. He reaches audiences online that sometimes rival the population of his home country. He also shoots almost entirely with his phone. "I found I was really encumbered," he says of his work with traditional broadcast gear. "I wanted to be like the radio journalists who would come along with a little backpack."

Figure CC1.2 Dougal Shaw.

Courtesy of Dougal Shaw

Maybe too many of us are encumbered, by not our gear but our notions of how broadcast journalism is supposed to look. Particularly in the States, most new J-school graduates seek small-market jobs on a path that seems preordained. Because Shaw entered the business in such a unique way – and, of course, in a different country with a different broadcast landscape – he didn't feel hemmed in by a particular path. He gravitated to what he liked. He learned that the BBC offered training seminars in various cameras and software, so he signed up. He found his quickest path to solo production would be through the Web, so he latched on. He discovered, even at an institution nearly a century old, an opportunity to ease onto the solo video highway.

"If you were just starting to use the camera," he says, "they might say, 'We're doing a story for the web site. Would you like to make a film to go with it?' So I was able to produce dozens of films, learning all of the things that can go wrong – and learning how to make my life easier."

Once Shaw switched to the phone, he flexed his autonomy further. He researched the necessary equipment and figured out a setup that works for mobile journalism. As phones evolve, so does his kit. When we spoke over Skype, Shaw said he uses a rig to hold the phone, attaches a broadcast-level microphone through an adapter, and occasionally adds a top light. And a tripod? Nah. He uses a pocket gimbal and leans on the stabilization feature in Final Cut X, Apple's marvelous editing software.

The digital explosion – in both equipment and media – has opened extraordinary avenues for one-person crews. It has also forced traditional titans to adapt. Shaw says the BBC isn't alone in embracing VJs: So do fellow British broadcasters ITV and Channel 4. So does RTE, the State broadcaster in Ireland, which invited Shaw to serve on a panel at its popular Mojofest, a once-annual global conference that itself illustrated the rise in video producers who can do it all.

Today, Shaw fills a role that seems hyper-designed for his sensibilities, but he mostly designed it himself. Much like Morgan, he entered a news agency that held thousands of employees along with undeveloped land in the form of solo video journalism.

"Even though you've learned to do the role of five people," Shaw muses, "you don't get paid as if you're five people. I've been offered jobs through LinkedIn to help with PR firms and advertising. Yeah, I could earn more money, but I wouldn't have the creative freedom."

That's why Shaw continues to align himself with – and even spearhead – the BBC's innovation efforts. He test-drives new equipment, from the iPhone to the 360-degree camera, and experiments with different modes of presentation. He even contributes to the BBC Academy Blog, where he outlines his "mojo diet" – mojo being the shorthand for mobile journalism.

He also fully embraces the potential – and challenges – of the solo mindset.

"It's mentally exhausting," Shaw says. "You're so tired after a shoot, even when physically you haven't done that much, because of all the concentrating you need to do. But I would never want to give it up because I love it so much. Every frame, every shot decision, everything is you."

On those nights crisscrossing the counties of northwest Iowa, I didn't just fall in love with the camera.

I also fell into burnout.

I struggled to find the energy for the 12-hour days and last-second finishes before air. I relied on adrenaline and determination, which can both be positive but not if they're your only drivers. Two months after receiving the title of sports director, I knocked on my news director's door and expressed concerns I had taken on too much. Eventually the spring arrived with its slower pace of sports coverage, and I caught my breath.

Many young MMJs don't. Many get out.

Throughout my first two jobs in local TV news, I befriended numerous colleagues who chose to walk away from aspirations they had held since college, high school, or earlier. Their reasons were almost always the same: they felt overworked and underappreciated, and they could not envision a career that replicated this path for the next four decades. I never judged. I certainly won't say they made the wrong choice. Broadcast news remains a brutal business where a small percentage of rookie reporters rise to a position of prestige, and it asks the most out of those of us who work alone.

But, unlike when I worked in Sioux City, it's no longer the only option.

Speaking with Morgan and Shaw, I gained an extra degree of faith in the path of the solo video journalist. Neither entered the business planning to use a camera – Shaw couldn't possibly have predicted using the camera on his phone – but both seemed remarkably content, even energized, by the possibilities that unfolded through their journeys and continue to appear today. They champion their solo status, and they have found powerful outlets through which to use it.

"I can't imagine not filming," Shaw told me. "It's too important to me."

And Morgan? "I don't see myself ever giving up shooting," she said. "I see a life where I will always have a camera."

Part II

In the Field

Shooting Video   5

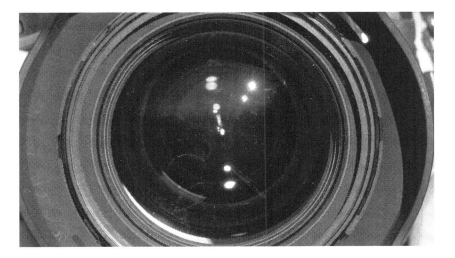

Figure 5.1
Credit: Matt Pearl

I get it.

For most would-be reporters learning the skills of solo video journalism, most of the profession seems like a giant Thanksgiving dinner of investigation, creativity, and excitement … and shooting one's own story seems like a side of broccoli.

It's the vegetable you need to eat but hate to digest.

My job, in the next few chapters, is to prove it's really a nice slice of pumpkin pie.

(If you don't like pumpkin pie, substitute whichever Thanksgiving-related dessert you enjoy. I am partial to my mother's cranberry mini-muffins …)

Before we get into the reasons why the best MMJs relish the opportunity to pick up the camera, let's list all the reasons – many of which make complete sense – why many MMJs abhor it:

Shooting is, physically, the most demanding part of the job. Journalism, for many, is a mental pursuit; it should not tax the body.

Shooting is mentally exhausting as well. It forces a one-person crew to balance both the technical steps of using a camera and the creative and information-gathering demands of developing a story.

Shooting is a blow to the ego. Particularly for solo video journalists in larger markets, it can be the source of mockery from traditional reporters and derision from traditional photographers. It is the part of the job that prevents them from striding around in expensive suits or dresses.

Shooting is a step with no finite conclusion. One cannot simply print a checklist of shots and collect them in the field. One must examine every situation and get as much footage as possible, never fully able to declare when the job is done.

Shooting alone almost always requires driving alone. Where a traditional reporter can work to develop his or her story – making phone calls, starting to write a script, or just relaxing in the passenger seat – an MMJ must keep two hands on the wheel.

Shooting is not fun.

Shooting is behind-the-scenes.

Shooting is not storytelling.

These reasons, for so many, can be summed up by one prevailing feeling:

Shooting is "not why I got into the business."

I know the feeling. I grew up wanting to be a play-by-play announcer for the NFL. I required enough technical know-how to push RECORD on a tape recorder. When I decided instead to become a sports anchor, I found I would not be able to get a job in most small markets without being able and willing to use a camera. I had never considered learning to shoot, and I had never envisioned it as part of my career.

As I said at the start, I get it.

But I completely disagree.

As a solo video journalist, I expend the most mental and physical energy while shooting. It is easily the most taxing part of my day. But I relish the chance to do it, and I understood long ago the advantages of being my own photographer:

Shooting gives me control. Traditional reporters return from the field with perhaps passing knowledge of what has been recorded, but I know exactly what I have captured, and I can often envision how I might write to and edit my footage.

Shooting offers creative freedom. I do not need to ask anyone's permission and convince a second person to take an aesthetic risk. If I want to capture a shot of a traffic light, I do not need to explain to a photographer why he or she should shoot it. I also do not need to apologize later if I don't use it.

Shooting streamlines the process. Throughout this book, you will hear me say how the best solo video journalists refuse to approach their jobs like assembly lines. We don't shoot, then write, then edit; we write and edit while we shoot, in a way that can be more difficult for traditional crews.

Shooting can be thrilling. I love the triumph of rolling on a beautiful moment, sensing in progress the majesty of what I am recording.

I will not lie and say shooting makes an MMJ's job easier. It does not. But it does make an MMJ's job far more empowering.

Shooting is fun.

Shooting is not just a behind-the-scenes job.

Shooting IS storytelling.

Anne Herbst does not label herself as a shooter.

She does not label herself as anything.

"I am definitely not a journalist to be put in any sort of box," says the Director of Visual Journalism at Denver's NBC affiliate, KUSA-TV.

Herbst (Figure 5.2) developed long ago a reputation as one of the top solo video journalists in the country. She mentors numerous younger MMJs and regularly speaks on the subject at conferences. But she refuses to fly the flag for one-person operations.

She would rather fly it for versatility.

"I think [working solo] makes me a better teammate when I'm on a team," she says. "I think it makes me a better employee. I do it to challenge myself. I do it because it's fun. I do it because it's a little different."

"But," she says, "I don't wear this as a badge of honor at all. It's just something that I do."

She happens to do it extremely well.

Figure 5.2 Anne Herbst.

Credit: Steve Gray

Herbst entered journalism school with the goal of reporting for a newspaper. When a professor told her she was better at shooting video, she re-routed and received an internship at KUSA.

"That place turned it around for me," she says. "I never wanted to do TV. I had no interest in TV. But they convinced me: 'You can write, but you can also shoot and do artistic stuff.'"

Throughout her career, Herbst has nourished those twin passions – as well as a third. Herbst founded the NPPA's Women in Visual Journalism conference and recently took over its Advanced Storytelling Workshop. She regularly provides critiques for younger MMJs – particularly women, who make up a large portion of the solo community but too infrequently receive speaking roles at conferences.

"People get all freaked out," Herbst says, "like, 'You're carrying that stuff all by yourself?' Conferences are weighted heavily towards men, and there needs to be a female perspective."

And what is Herbst's perspective on the one-person work she sees? She can often tell something's missing.

"A lot of young MMJs want to be reporters," Herbst says. "They don't want to be photographers. And I can really see it. They aren't able to get great moments to write great stories, because they don't really care about it. And you miss a lot of great stuff if that's your motivation."

But when you get that great stuff? You leave with a satisfied smile.

"It's all yours, and it feels so good," she says. "You feel really accomplished. There are some really tiring, exhausting things about being an MMJ, but there are some great things."

Before we delve into those great things, let's master the techniques that provide a foundation.

Understanding the Basics

The "foundation," in this case, does not refer to the true foundations of shooting: how to focus, zoom, open and close the iris, white balance, and press RECORD.

In this case, it refers to the essential building blocks of visual storytelling. Far too often, solo video journalists fail to use them.

In fact, if I had to point to one thing missing from most stories by young one-woman and one-man bands, I would not need long to determine my answer:

Sequences.

Learn to properly shoot and then edit sequences, and you will immediately leap forward as a storyteller.

It's a simple step. It involves getting shots of the same subject or action from multiple zoom lengths. Shots typically fall into one of three aptly-named categories:

- Wide shots: These are your establishing shots, which allow you to set the scene and allow your viewer to get a sense of, physically, where your story takes place.
- Medium shots: These are your substantive shots, zoomed close enough to capture your subject but wide enough to indicate some distance.
- Tight shots: These are your dramatic shots, where you show little else but a specific item or portion of your subject.

How does this work in practice? Let's say you are filming a conversation between two people on the street. The wide shot would capture the people in the context of the street; the medium shot would show the people themselves, perhaps from the waist up; and the tight shot would focus on one person's face (for another example, see Figures 5.3, 5.4 and 5.5).

How does this improve your storytelling? Most importantly, it establishes continuity. You must always keep in mind that a viewer has not experienced your story like you have. You might spend several hours on a shoot and

Figures 5.3, 5.4 and 5.5 Ideally your story will be about something more
active than flowers in the park.

Credit: Matt Pearl

capture 30 minutes of video, but a viewer will only see 90 seconds of it, often
compressed into 20 or 30 actual shots. That means you must constantly,
within your story, reestablish its location and provide a clear path for your
audience to follow.

From a visual sense, sequences provide that path. You can edit them in
various ways – start with a wide shot and follow with a medium and several
tights, or start with a tight shot and then back up with a wide – but by using
them you create a far more digestible story.

You also, as a solo act, make your job much easier.

"You're shooting sequences because they are really easy to edit together,"
says Herbst. "I make sure I get enough wides and tights. Mediums are great,
but wides and tights will get you around a lot of stuff. You want those shots
to help get you out of jams."

Beyond that, a proper sequence can provide triple or quadruple the bang
for your photographic buck. Let's say you use, in a typical story, 30 shots.
Without sequences, you must find and capture a unique moment for each

of those shots; that means 30 moments. With sequences, you can capture the same moment with three shots from different distances or zoom lengths. That means you only need to find ten unique moments.

The numbers speak the truth: sequences are golden.

Even more golden? Using a tripod.

Younger MMJs often despise the tripod. It is bulky, difficult to carry, and seemingly unnecessary. After all, one does not need a tripod to record video. One only requires a camera.

But one almost always needs a tripod to record steady video.

A tripod is, at its most fundamental level, the difference between TV news and home movies. It enables stable, balanced video that can rarely be achieved without one. Especially when getting shots that require a heavy zoom, a photographer benefits greatly from having a firm base on which to plant the camera.

"Mostly I shoot on a tripod," Herbst says. "If I move, I carry the whole thing attached. I do it all the time. It's better to be on the tripod all the time than on the ground."

I didn't always feel that way.

During my junior year of college, I received a three-month internship at KELO-TV, the top-rated station in Sioux Falls, South Dakota. I often shot sports, where I never used a tripod because I needed to capture fast-moving action, but the assignment editors would occasionally ask me to shoot a news story. One wintry weekend, they sent me to the scene of a car accident on an icy highway. I arrived and got out of my news van, only to get pelted by repeated blasts of wind and snow. I could barely keep my balance. I decided, instead of using two hands to carry both the camera and tripod, I would take only the camera and leave my left hand free to potentially break a fall.

I did not fall, but I did not record anything close to usable video.

That night KELO-TV aired a shaky, potentially seasickness-inducing mess. At the next day's morning meeting, while discussing a potential follow-up piece, the chief photographer belted two sentences that stung so much I remember them today:

"Hey, do we have any good video of that? Any tripod-ed video?"

Everyone got quiet. My face got red.

No one in the meeting stood up for me. Perhaps the chief had crossed the line by humiliating an intern, but he was not wrong. And I have never forgotten his lesson. You can spare yourself a similar one by getting comfortable with your tripod. It's true that many documentaries and TV shows today rely on footage shot without one, but their photographers typically use rigs and stabilizers that most broadcast journalists don't possess. Particularly in the early stages of your career, you can eliminate an enormous variable – the potential shakiness of a shot – by taking a few extra seconds to set up your sticks.

You can also help yourself enormously by knowing your gear as well as possible. You should "feel like the camera is a part of your body," Herbst says.

Why?

"The technical part of it is really daunting for a lot of people. If there's a technical glitch, I need to know how to fix it and not get all freaked out in front of the people I'm interviewing. I need to be able to fix it while I'm talking to them about their dog. I need to be able to multi-task, fix my gear, and have a chat with these people so they don't feel like I'm wasting their time."

On a theoretical level, most photographers understand they will likely face the occasional technical hiccup, from a static-filled microphone signal, to a dead battery, to a loose tripod leg.

When such hiccups occur, the best photographers – and, thus, the best MMJs – know how to troubleshoot with composure.

That comes by understanding your equipment – and, sadly, learning from experience. I have reached a point where I have faced and conquered virtually every issue that can arise in the field. When one happens now, I can rely on steps that have worked in the past.

If you have not reached that point, you can at least remember to field adversity with serenity.

Capturing People

Let's go back a few paragraphs to an example worthy of elaboration.

When Herbst faces a technical glitch, she says, she must "be able to fix it while I'm talking to [the people I'm interviewing] about their dog."

The underlying point? A journalist must be able to do her or his job while calling as little attention to it as possible.

"It's everyone's goal, right?" says Herbst. "'Just forget that we're here.' They can't just forget that we're here."

They also cannot forget about the camera that can potentially capture their every move and immortalize it on television. The camera, in a fundamental way, serves as a major barrier to authenticity – which is, of course, all a journalist really wants.

In a traditional news crew, the reporter can often distract people from the photographer's actions. Some of the best reporters I know are also the most disarming. They connect with their interview subjects seemingly immediately, and they enable those subjects to become comfortable with being on camera. The photographer can then capture those coveted authentic moments that elevate a story.

A one-person crew must juggle both jobs, which often requires juggling multiple personalities: the focused journalist and the empathetic human being.

That means avoiding the pitfalls that make an already artificial situation seem more so.

Step 1 (and it is worthy of all caps): NO STAGING!

"I think the biggest piece of advice is to not tell anyone what to do," says Herbst. "I never ask anyone to stop, and I never ask anyone to slow down." Why? "You're not a director. You're a journalist."

But when a situation develops quickly or feels overwhelming, a frazzled shooter can lose sight of that. He or she may attempt to slow things down by trying to guide the situation. That simply does not work, from either an ethical sense or a storytelling one.

Of course, a photographer often encounters gray areas. For example, perhaps you have just been assigned to cover a mother who says her son was wrongly suspended for fighting in school. You call the mother, who agrees to an interview at home. You arrive and conduct the interview (a process we will cover in full in the next chapter), but you cannot leave with just that. You must shoot B-roll, or footage to show under your tracked audio.

What should you do? You cannot simply point your camera and start rolling, because you will only obtain B-roll of a dumbfounded mother, staring at you with a look that says, "Are you serious?"

Should you stage something?

Not exactly.

But you can establish potential B-roll situations before you arrive and then allow your subjects to execute them.

"I'll get to know a little bit about them before I get there," says Herbst. "I try to know what I'm in for. I'm always doing homework on people, if that makes sense."

And if, during that homework, Herbst discovers an activity germane to her piece, she will tell her interviewees she wishes to capture it.

For example, she once told the story of a husband, Jack Cohen, who donated part of his liver to his wife, Ruth. Talking with them on the phone, Herbst struggled to figure out a possibility for B-roll ... until she learned how Jack pushed wheelchair-bound Ruth on daily walks around the block. She jumped at the opportunity and asked Ruth and Jack when they would walk next.

That became a precious supply of B-roll when Herbst sat down to edit.

"That story is so visually poor," she says, "but it's one of my favorites, because I was able to, as a one-man band, jump through so many freaking hoops to get that thing done."

One hoop that often seems daunting is obtaining great audio from your interview subjects. Again, I am not referring to generating responses during a formal interview setting; I will cover that in Chapter 6. I am focusing specifically on B-roll situations, which can often produce tremendous nuggets of sound.

Those nuggets come far more easily when you provide your interviewee with a wireless lavaliere microphone.

Considering how many people freeze up around a camera, a solo video journalist might expect a similar response to wearing a wireless microphone. And one might receive that response … at first.

"When you convince someone to do an interview, the mic is so invasive," Herbst says. "But once you get it on [the person], then it's fine! Then it's just a conversation."

Or, more bluntly, "Most people forget about it the minute you stop shoving the microphone in their butt pocket."

This, in my experience, is quite true. I cannot tell you how many times I have needed, at the end of a shoot, to remind my subject that she or he is still wearing a microphone. Today's wireless mics weigh very little and feel surprisingly natural. My advice? Follow the famous slogan for Ron Popeil's Showtime Rotisserie: set it and forget it.

Then make sure you hear the results by wearing headphones when you shoot. You want to be aware of every sound imprinted on your memory card, and you will not always be in a position to hear with your ears, particularly as you walk away for wider shots.

I once told the story of William Lowary, a rock climber who took part in the World Championships of Paraclimbing. William is blind, and when I came over to his home for our first shoot, he seemed visibly tentative. At one point, he leaned toward his mother and whispered something I would not have heard without headphones:

"It's very weird," William said, "having someone film me."

That moment – an endearing, sweet two seconds that helped introduce William's personality – found a fitting home at the start of my story.

The best one-person crews know how to establish an environment where those moments happen naturally. They understand the Golden Rule of solo shooting, articulated beautifully by Herbst:

"Just act like a normal human being. Don't act all reporter-ly."

Gathering Material

Of course, photographers should still think all reporter-ly. They might not conduct the interviews or write the story, but the best ones communicate with their reporters about collecting video that fits the yet-to-be-written script.

An MMJ must do this internally … and that's a major advantage.

Because television relies on strong visuals, a solo video journalist must focus on both gathering information and obtaining B-roll that fits with it. This means, most importantly, shooting with a purpose: seeking out compelling shots that advance the story.

I advocated in Chapter 1 for taking a brief chunk of time, after receiving one's assignment, to brainstorm it: Why does this story matter? What video do I need to make that point to the viewer? How can I go beyond the norm?

I thus arrive at my shoot with a greater sense of focus – an important quality when dealing with the circus of uncertainty that comes with the newsgathering process. I try to avoid collecting shots that show no immediate connection to my story.

On the flip side, when I detect a shot that could fit perfectly, I will devote massive amounts of energy – and sometimes time – to ensure I get it right (Figure 5.6).

Figure 5.6 For the right story, this shot could be worth a five-minute wait.

Credit: Matt Pearl

Herbst does the same thing. I believe it's her defining trait as a photojournalist: her willingness to wait for that perfect moment if she senses it might be worth it.

"I have waited five minutes for a bird to fly up off of a post," she says.

"I am not afraid to burn space, if I have a little time, to get that moment. You need that memorable stuff in your story ... not that the bird flying off the post is memorable, but maybe it's what the bird was reacting to!"

"But," she adds, "while I'm waiting for the bird to fly away, as a one-man band, I'm writing; I'm multi-tasking."

Exactly. You cannot shoot with purpose unless you think, while shooting, about your writing. Similar to how one captures individual shots with the expectation of editing them later into a sequence, one must also look for B-roll that matches a potential script. You never want to write a story before you shoot it; you should approach each piece with an open mind and willingness to learn. But you can certainly brainstorm, both in advance and during a shoot. You can think of potential lines or turns of phrase, and you can figure out ways in the field to represent them visually.

You can also make notes, both mentally and physically, of potential shots and sound bites you want to include.

"When I get a sound bite that I like, I just flip up bars," says Herbst, referring to a function common on most cameras that records a rainbow of color bars and a screechy tone. That way, when she looks later through a sea of B-roll and interviews, she can quickly identify those pivotal sound bites. Other journalists use a far lower-tech option: they put one of their hands over the lens so, after they record a moment they like, they follow it with nothing but black. Others use their phones: they snap a photo of their viewfinder with the shot in question, and, if time allows, post it on social media – one way of engaging their digital audience while their story is still forming.

"I'm doing everything on the fly," says Herbst. "Usually the story is almost written by the time I get back to the station."

This is especially true if she is able to capture great audio, and not just from people.

Every so often, I will hear a photographer expound, "Great audio is even more important than great video." I don't know if I fully believe that; one cannot tell a story without video, making it, in my mind, more essential. But I definitely understand the thinking.

Audio is what allows a storyteller to fully immerse a viewer in a story's environment. A photographer must, in the field, seek two types of audio: general, atmospheric sound that goes under the reporter's tracks, and specific natural bursts that fit between those tracks and sound bites. Those bursts are usually called NAT pops.

Obtaining atmospheric sound is relatively easy: just make sure your camera or shotgun microphone is picking up audio when you shoot. Then, when you edit, you can lay down a video clip at the same time as its corresponding audio.

Finding NAT pops is tougher – and a frequently forgotten task by photographers who don't think to do it.

What constitutes a NAT pop? It can be anything short, grabbing, and loud. Here is a quick list of examples you have probably heard, if not on the news then in the movies:

- The whirr of a car driving down the street
- The buzz of a chainsaw cutting through a fallen tree
- The snap of a baseball into a catcher's mitt
- The implosion of a building
- The explosion of a firework
- The explosion of a gas tank
- The explosion of anything.

The next time you find yourself in public, set aside a minute to stand still and listen for NAT pops. You will probably hear half a dozen.

Keep that mindset on a shoot, and you can capture some great moments.

If I notice a NAT pop worth getting, I try to put a wireless microphone as close as possible to the source of the sound. This enables me to isolate that sound, which is critical in noisy environments.

I needed this technique on a shoot in 2014, at the Winter Olympics in Sochi.

I was reporting about the most popular structure in the central village: a larger-than-life-size construction of the Olympic rings. A giant line of visitors would gather every day around the rings, all ready to pose for photos. Spectators would step up on the structure's base, always making the same loud noise with their shoes:

STOMP, STOMP.

I knew I wanted to capture that sound.

I also knew I could not do so with my shotgun microphone.

Surrounding the rings were numerous speakers, all blaring the latest hits of Top 40 radio. I could not have snared the STOMP, STOMP without a large helping of Nicki Minaj lyrics … unless I got right next to it.

I tucked my lavaliere microphone on the corner of the base, then used my headphones to make sure I picked up the sound I wanted. Sure enough, people continued to stomp, and I captured it.

When using any of these techniques, I think about one overarching goal: capturing moments that viewers will remember.

"How do I recognize a moment?" says Herbst. "It makes me feel something."

Watch any story that moves you, and you will likely be able to pick out the moments. Shoot any story worth telling, and you should notice them in the field. Your job, then, is to spot them and get video.

When talking with Herbst, she brought up a story she shot about a legitimate concern for many Coloradans:

Bears.

Specifically, bears coming too close to people's homes, thanks to easy access to their trash cans.

Herbst produced a story about companies that sold bear-proof trash cans and tested them with actual bears. She went to a facility and shot one of these tests, snaring a great moment where a bear (in a glass cage, mind you) arrived upon a trash can and absolutely mauled it.

"I only had 12 minutes to get that bear decimating that trash can," she recalls. "So I knew, 'I have to stay on top of my game here.'"

That meant a few things:

*   Holding shots longer to fully capture the standout moments.
*   Getting a series of shots from multiple zoom lengths, so she could show the moments as sequences in the edited story.
*   Anticipating how the decimation might unfold – and staying alert for actions that defied her expectations.

Of course, moments are not always so predictable.

"I miss stuff a lot," says Herbst with a laugh. "You're gonna miss stuff. You're gonna miss moments. But once you get the moment you love – that happens within frame – you can allow yourself to move on."

And you can put together a story that's far more memorable.

Shooting with Smarts

But you also need to shoot the video that gets you from Point A to Point B, or Moment A to Moment B.

Sometimes it doesn't need to be video you shot … or video, period.

A solo video journalist should think of every available visual option to help properly tell a story, and that sometimes means gathering viewer-generated photos and video. I have used this strategy on countless pieces, from day turns to long-form packages.

I can think of no better example than a story about a powerful pair of moments at a Little League baseball game.

A viewer had written us about Andrew Williams, an 11-year-old who loved the sport of baseball, largely because of his father. Greg Williams had served as his children's coach and had always made time to play catch in the yard. The previous summer, Greg had been diagnosed with Lou Gehrig's disease, or ALS. He had held on for nearly a year but passed away June 3rd, less than two weeks before Father's Day.

On that meaningful holiday, Andrew played in a Little League game and did something far beyond the norm:

He hit two home runs … in honor of his dad.

When I read about Andrew's homers, I felt chills. I still get chills when I think about it today. I produced a story that won numerous honors, from a Southeast Regional Emmy to a Regional Edward R. Murrow Award to an NPPA Best of Photojournalism Award.

But I could not have told such a poignant story if I had not obtained video of the home runs.

Before I set up any interviews for Andrew's story, I focused on tracking down a usable recording. So many people shoot video with their cell phones, especially at their children's sporting events, and I assumed I could find a clip of Andrew's homers if I asked enough people.

I assumed right, and I got the video I needed.

But I also concentrated on obtaining photos, namely of Andrew's father. For obvious reasons, I would not be able to show any present-day video of Greg, but I knew his family would likely possess numerous snapshots – both by himself and with his wife and kids. Those photos proved critical in thoroughly telling the Williams' story.

I take these steps for not just potential award-winners but virtually every story I do. I constantly inquire about photos to help fill the gaps in my stories, and I often use those photos – even ones that don't make the final story – in posts on Facebook and Instagram. I highly recommend it.

I also recommend seeking and shooting cutaways, which Herbst calls by a different name.

"I shoot 10 to 15 'cover-my-ass' shots," she says: "tight shots that will get me out of any sort of jam. They always have something to do with the story, but they're not the most active shots. They are the shots that will save my butt in the end."

You might reasonably wonder why your butt might need saving. As with many of the techniques in this chapter, this one deals with continuity.

While you largely want to spray your story with sequences, you will likely reach several points while editing where you simply need to fill a hole. For example, you cannot cut from a medium shot of a police chief to another medium shot of the chief; doing so will break the continuity of your police-based story.

We call that a "jump cut," because you have made an edit that clearly jumps ahead or behind in time.

Here is where you can reach for a cutaway, which looks exactly as it sounds: it is a shot away from the action, usually on the tighter side, that allows you to move forward in your story without breaking the space–time continuum. For your police story, a cutaway might be a super-tight shot of the chief's badge or the flashing lights of his or her patrol car.

When Herbst mentions the need to capture 10–15 of these, she emphasizes another key philosophy of shooting: overshoot, don't undershoot. I have been shooting my own stories for nearly two decades, but I can only recall a handful of packages where I did not, at some point while editing, wish I had shot more B-roll.

You can almost never shoot too much. You must eventually cut yourself off in order to set out on the rest of your day, but you should use whatever time you can to fill your visual cup with footage.

The Final Foundations

I close this chapter with two critical pieces of advice.

First and foremost, be safe. The process of shooting a story can occasionally place journalists in potentially dangerous situations, none of which should be approached without understanding the risks and, if necessary, raising one's voice.

"Safety is huge," Herbst says, particularly for those who work alone. "It's a little terrifying to go out at midnight on a freaking gang shooting. It's terrifying for anybody!"

Solo video journalists face the unenviable task of carrying a bunch of heavy, delicate, expensive gear, with no one nearby to call 911 in case of an emergency. I have never been shy about speaking up when I feel I am being sent to an abnormally unsafe situation. I encourage all one-person crews to take similar stances.

"I've had some threatening stuff happen when I'm out by myself," Herbst says, "and I get in my car and I leave." Herbst is a renowned photojournalist who routinely expends extra effort for her stories, but she does not risk her life for them. She stresses this point constantly with female MMJs, who, she says, may feel an extra sense of danger in certain situations.

Regardless of gender, you should never be afraid to say you're afraid.

You should also never be afraid to take chances and be creative.

Throughout this chapter I have explored a variety of techniques. Nearly all can make your story better, but they can also make it stale and boring without compelling subjects and innovative vision. The best photographers do not just follow the rules; they build upon them and bend them. When the right moment strikes, they even break them.

Remember, this is the fun part! This is where you get to set the tone for your story's appearance, and you are unbound in how you do it. Solo video journalists who embrace the aesthetic nature of the job – shooting from different angles, using multiple (and super-small) cameras, finding creative ways to capture a subject – enjoy themselves far more. They relish the chance to seize visual control from start to finish, and they find ways to elevate each story with a unique approach.

"It's easier to be lazy when you're by yourself," says Herbst. "But it's also easier to go overboard."

Do it.

Go overboard … to a point, of course. Leave room for writing, editing, posting, and more.

But don't look at shooting as a necessary evil. Appreciate the opportunity, and take advantage of the power it provides.

Shooting Interviews 6

Figure 6.1

Credit: Matt Pearl

In the second season of one of the most popular TV shows of all time, Jerry Seinfeld opened an episode with a classic piece of stand-up comedy about advertising.

Specifically, he said at the start of the *Seinfeld* episode, "The Phone Message," he loved to laugh at the people in soda commercials.

"Where do they summon this enthusiasm?" Seinfeld mused. "Have you seen them? 'We have soda! We have soda!' [They're] jumping, laughing, flying through the air … it's a can of soda!"

He then raised a scenario that, I swear, has played out multiple times in my life.

"Have you ever been watching TV and you're drinking the exact product they're advertising right there on TV? And they're spiking volleyballs … [there's] girls in bikinis … and I'm standing there like, 'Maybe I put too much ice in mine'" (David & Seinfeld, 1991).

Sadly, I feel this way not just when I drink soda but, far too often, when I conduct interviews.

When I sit in the newsroom and make phone calls about a story, I cannot help but imagine the possibilities. I reach someone who overflows with passion and wows me with a firm stance and willingness to make powerful statements. I jump at the chance to interview this person. I salivate at the opportunity for head-turning sound bites that will force even the most casual viewer to focus on my story. I envision a true "We have soda!" experience.

Then I meet the person and start the interview, and I wonder if I have put too much ice in it.

People simply act much differently on camera, particularly when they are being interviewed. Their instincts kick in, and they realize their words will suddenly become permanent – able to be parsed, refuted, and potentially edited in a way they did not intend.

I completely understand. To be honest, knowing everything I know about television news, I doubt I would easily agree to be on the receiving end of an interview … unless I trusted the person conducting it.

The best interviewers know how to quickly develop trust, comfort, and authenticity with their subjects. They receive organic and honest responses, by not extracting them but enabling them through natural situations and a pleasant demeanor.

Of course, as a solo act, you must develop this relaxed rapport while managing the Constitution-length checklist in your head. You must figure out the best interview setting, frame your shot, check your lighting, and keep an ear on your audio. You must handle any technical mishaps and remain unfazed if your interview subject does not immediately offer the sound bites you desire. You must remember which questions you plan to ask and which topics you plan to address, and you cannot forget to stay focused on the answers and actively think of strong follow-ups.

Boyd Huppert, a renowned feature reporter for KARE-TV in the Twin Cities, once gave a beautiful presentation about interviewing called "The

Dance." The title refers to the nonverbal communication between a reporter and photographer required to develop a comfortable interview setting while gathering the necessary footage and sound bites. The video of this presentation is, at last check, still available on YouTube; it is a must-watch for aspiring TV journalists.

It also gave birth to this quote from a trailblazing solo video journalist:

"When you can dance with yourself, that's when you know you've got it down."

The man behind that quote is one of the best dancers around.

When deciding who to interview for this book, I mandated I would only speak with current working solo video journalists, because I wanted to ensure the advice given was relevant to today's MMJs.

Mitch Pittman (Figure 6.2) is a necessary exception.

I interviewed Pittman in 2015 when I wrote the original edition of *The Solo Video Journalist*. At the time he was a flourishing soloist at KOMO-TV in Seattle, where he remained until September 2018. That's when he became Director of Photography at Side Road Media, where he continues his prowess with the camera. I thought about replacing him for this chapter, but then I reread the chapter. I decided I couldn't.

Pittman's advice was too darn good.

Figure 6.2 Mitch Pittman.

Courtesy of Mitch Pittman

"We do have something to prove," he told me at the time. "At most of the shops where I have worked, I have been the first MMJ to be there. All eyes are on you. There's a lot of pressure, and you want to perform your best."

Pittman never minded the pressure. "I think it's OK," he said, "because it drives you."

During his early jobs as a one-man band – first at the FOX affiliate in Burlington, Vt., then at the ABC affiliate in Minneapolis/St. Paul – Pittman relished the occasions when he wound up on the same story as a competitor's two-person crew. By 2013, the 2009 college grad had won a trifecta of regional Emmy awards. He blossomed into one of the country's best young – and best, period – solo video journalists.

His stories specialized in creatively shot and powerfully conducted interviews. He routinely changed his shots mid-question and collected various angles of his subjects. As a result, his stories always felt visually exciting while still containing those arrow-to-the-heart sound bites that stay with a viewer long after the final frame.

Unsurprisingly, Pittman approaches the do-it-all challenges of interviews with a two-word mentality: no excuses.

In 2014 he wrote a guest post for the TV News Storytellers blog entitled, "The Nuances of an MMJ Interview." He used the space to debunk every reason why a one-person crew, in theory, should not be able to produce engaging, aesthetically diverse interviews. Pittman concluded the article thus:

> Every MMJ knows there's no greater compliment than when someone sees you reporting a story and asks, "Who shot that?" If you keep these techniques in mind, you'll find your stories not just looking as good as a two-person team, but BETTER.
>
> (Pittman, 2014)

Why did he write it?

"I feel like there's a perception of, 'Oh, you're an MMJ? So you're just gonna shoot it in one spot, have a medium shot, and it's gonna be static.'"

"People have a low expectation, and they shouldn't."

Setting up the Interview

Of course, before you can defy the skeptics and naysayers with a myriad of interview angles, you must first accomplish a far more basic task – or, perhaps, a deceptively basic one:

Create an environment for openness.

During the last chapter, I stressed the importance of authenticity and discussed strategies for achieving it when collecting B-roll. Many of the same tools apply to interviews. In fact, they become more critical because the interview typically occurs first.

This, by the way, is not set in stone. You might choose or be forced to shoot footage before you conduct your interview, and you might find the approach more helpful. I typically judge each situation by whatever I believe will produce the most natural moments in both cases. I also consider questions of logistics and time.

For example, when I arrive at the scene of a protest, I take a few minutes to feel out the sensitivity of the situation. I try to determine who will be most willing to talk, most authorized to speak about the event, and least affected by the artifice of the camera. If I expect to face a tight deadline at the protest's end, I will record a few interviews beforehand, which I might do anyway so I can later write and edit my story with a chronological flow. But I typically prefer to capture natural sound of any speakers and then wait to conduct interviews until afterward, when the protesters and leaders can reflect on what they just did.

Similarly, when I am assigned to cover a vigil of some sort, I mostly hold back until it ends. I try to respect the raw emotion of events like these, and I would rather allow those involved to get used to my presence from a distance before I approach them for interviews.

In many situations, though, I choose to conduct the interview first. I try to ease my interview subjects into the situation, and I believe they will feel less awkward answering questions on camera than performing actions. More fundamentally, the interview is typically a much higher priority for my story. If I am assigned to get reaction from an embattled mayor, my news director far prefers me to land the interview rather than collect B-roll.

In any event, one must establish the proper environment for an interview long before pressing RECORD.

"I think the interview really starts when you come to the door and say hi," Pittman says, "because it all leads to your getting better sound and making it more natural for [your interview subject]. It's super-weird to be interviewed. People so often say, 'What questions are you going to ask?' I never want it to be formulated, so I never tell them what the questions are going to be."

Rather, Pittman tries "to give a piece of myself, because they are going to give a lot to me. [I think about] making a personal connection."

Of course, you must attempt to conjure this connection while figuring out and setting up your shot.

Many young MMJs never learn the proper way to light an interview, and it shows. I compare it to how I described shooting sequences in the last chapter: it is such an underdeveloped skill, but it is easy to learn and makes a critical difference.

The idea is to frame your interview subject so that her or his face is the brightest part of the shot. You also want to create a sense of separation between your interviewee's face and the background.

Figure 6.3 shows how that looks in practice.

In a traditionally lit interview, a photographer will bathe the majority of a subject's face in light while leaving the back sliver shaded. You can see it in my face here; I pop off the screen because of how and where the light shines.

How is this done? You need only remember two steps:

1. Determine your primary light source.
2. When conducting the interview, stand between that primary light source and your camera.

When I use the phrase "primary light source," I refer to whatever is providing the greatest amount of light in your interview setting. If you are outside, you can easily pick out that source: it's the sun. You can then ideally position your subject to look towards the sun but not directly at it, as in the photo below.

Figure 6.3 You can always find a source of light.

Credit: Matt Pearl

Finding a primary light source in an indoor setting can be tougher. Sometimes you will find yourself in a room with great natural light, usually from a giant window. Pittman prefers this approach when possible: "If you can use natural light, that means there's no light in someone's face. That's always one less thing that would make the person more nervous or clam up."

Many rooms fail to offer this option. They feature few, if any, windows and rely on electric lights that point down from the ceiling, which is the most functional spot to fill a room but provides the least flattering shine for an interview subject.

In these situations, I prefer to bring my own light.

I almost always carry my backpack to indoor interviews, and I have reached the point where I can usually set up a pair of lights in less than five minutes. I focus mostly on creating a setting that feels unobtrusive for my interviewee. When I used traditional bulbs, I would point my light away from the person and reflect it back by attaching a special umbrella. This provided a diffused, softer glow. It also made my interview subject feel less like he or she was on the receiving end of an interrogation. These days I use LED lights that achieve this effect on their own, without the umbrella. If you can corral one at your station, try to do so.

Again, when you sit down (or stand up) for the interview, you want to position yourself between the camera and the primary light source, as in the crude but effective drawing in Figure 6.4.

One does not always need to adhere to standard two-point lighting. Rules are, after all, made to be broken. But particularly in indoor situations, this rule almost always works best.

It is not, though, the only rule to keep in mind.

Specifically, one should obey the "rule of thirds" when framing an interview. This involves mentally dividing the viewfinder into a Tic-Tac-Toe board and positioning an interviewee where the gridlines meet. Many newer cameras come with a display setting that shows this grid in the viewfinder, as seen in Figure 6.5.

Rarely will a photojournalist frame an interview subject in the center of the screen. Instead, she or he will place the subject slightly off-center, with that person speaking not directly at the camera but across it to a reporter on the side.

But how, as a one-person crew, do you keep your interview subject in one place?

In my experience, people do not like standing still. Next time you have a conversation with someone where both of you are standing, pay attention to how frequently you both move around. You might barely notice if you don't

Figure 6.4 This setup works in virtually any room you can find.

Credit: Matt Pearl

Figure 6.5 Most smartphones come with the option of showing 3x3 gridlines in their camera apps.

Credit: Matt Pearl

look for it. MMJs constantly find themselves at the whims of their interviewees' movements, particularly if they choose a tight frame for their subjects.

Pittman always sizes up the other person before setting up his shot.

"I'm seeing how much they have a tendency to wiggle around," he says, especially "if it's someone who has never been on camera before. I want to make sure they're going to stay in the frame."

You can use one of several tactics to do this:

- Sit the person down, preferably in a chair that does not roll or rock. A simple seat with a straight back can be a solo video journalist's best friend.
- Position yourself to be able to see your viewfinder. This applies if you use a camera with a flip-screen, which you traditionally find on its left side, or a display monitor like most DSLR and mirrorless cameras. You simply seat yourself slightly behind your camera, which enables you to regularly check the framing while shooting a textbook-perfect interview.
- Frame your interview in a wider shot, particularly if you want to stand in a spot where you will not be able to see the viewfinder. If you want a tighter shot, you can always zoom digitally with your editing software.

You should also, whenever possible, try to place your interview subject in an appropriate surrounding. Interviewing a mechanic? Do it in the shop. Interviewing a cashier about Black Friday shopping? Do it at the register. When those opportunities do not present themselves, look for a background that is visually interesting but does not detract from the interview or put your subject in an unrelated context.

(For example, don't interview the mechanic behind a register on Black Friday.)

Regardless, you should aim to give yourself the fewest possible reasons for worry, because you want to focus most of your during-the-interview energy on the interview itself. So get comfortable with your camera, and wear headphones – at least at the start of the interview – to ensure you receive proper audio. You do not want to return to the station to find a beautifully shot piece of video with fuzzy, hissy audio – or, if you forgot to turn on the microphone, no audio at all.

Starting Wide, Then Going in Tight (Interviewer Edition)

Interviews come in all sizes, from two minutes with a passerby on the street to 30 minutes with the main subject of a longer package.

But the rhythm of interviews – most revealing interviews, anyway – rarely changes.

Pittman always starts with the same question.

"Every single interview," he says, "I'm like, 'What's going on here? Why are we here?'"

Steal it. Go ahead. Use it on every interview you conduct. Pittman won't mind. He learned long ago the benefit of starting with a softball.

"It's a good establishing question," he says, "but it's also an easy question for them and gets them comfortable. You don't want to start with the most in-depth questions. You want to ease them into it."

This advice is absolutely correct, and it also offers a stealthy advantage.

Have you ever watched a presidential debate, particularly one that jumped right into the moderator's questions without allowing for opening statements? The candidates almost always ignore the first question, using their time instead to give the very opening statement they were supposed to avoid. They do this because they want to frame the debate on their terms and recite their overarching talking points. They have something to say, and they will say it even if they must blow off the moderator's question.

Regular civilians often do the same.

They, like practiced politicians, want to use their interviews to make specific points. If you do not give them an easy, early opportunity to do so, they may try to shoehorn those points throughout the conversation.

I cannot imagine an easier invitation than, "Why are we here?" Once the subject has made her or his pivotal remarks, you can both move inward, so to speak, to deeper topics.

But when you do, try your best to take your time.

Solo video journalists feel the need to rush through their days, mainly because they feel the pressure of a seemingly endless number of responsibilities and deadlines. I understand the impulse, but I fight it hard during an interview. I want my subject to feel as if I have no other priority than to listen to what he or she has to say. Some people need little prodding to share their emotions and opinions, but most will not feel comfortable unloading their deepest thoughts after two or three minutes. They want to feel the attention and recognition of their interviewers, and they want to be sure those interviewers will be faithful stewards of their insights.

I always try to provide that attention, and I don't mind burning a few extra minutes if I can then capture more meaningful sound bites and emotions. An intern once told me I spend more time with my interviews than most traditional reporters, which surprised me because I typically possess fewer minutes to spare. But, I think, the extra investment pays off.

Remember: sound bites are your currency. You want to amass as many great ones as you can.

That also requires asking questions that seek emotion, not information.

Let me preface this by exclaiming the importance in any story of facts and details. You need to get them right, and you need to devote time in your workday to collecting the correct information about your story and then confirming those facts in your script.

But when the camera is rolling on an interview, you want to focus on feelings.

"If there are facts in a sound bite," says Pittman, "I never use them … because I can say them faster."

Powerful stories often thrive on human connections, which usually occur when the individuals in those stories allow themselves to be vulnerable.

When I think of vulnerability, I think of Dave Peterson.

In the summer of 2015, two months after nine people were murdered at Emanuel AME Church in Charleston, Peterson chose to go for a ride.

A motorcycle ride.

From Atlanta to Charleston.

With dozens of fellow bikers.

Sensing a racial divide in his own community – and seeing the racist hate at the center of the murders in Charleston – Peterson decided to connect his mostly white motorcycle group with a mostly black group in the next county. They organized a 300-mile ride under the name "Engines for Emanuel" (pictured in Figure 6.6).

Peterson possessed enormous passion, but when we sat down for his main interview, he struggled to express it. He seemed cautious, trying to remain politically correct and keep from saying the wrong thing.

Roughly 25 minutes into the interview, Peterson finally let out his emotions … with one of the most powerful sound bites I have ever heard.

"It's a show of support," he began when I asked why the ride mattered so much. "It's a reverence and solemnness for their loss to say, 'We are so sorry … for what happened.'"

Peterson's voice cracked, and he began to cry.

"Sorry," he told me before continuing.

"And it doesn't have to be that way," he went on, with a yearning and frustration that seemed to force its way to the surface. "We can come together," he said through stifled tears, "and we have the people around us

Figure 6.6 The team from Engines for Emanuel.

Courtesy of Jim Harrell

to show you we stand with you ... and we love you ... and things can be different" (Pearl, 2015).

I don't know how Peterson's words appear on paper, but years later I can still feel the sincerity and vulnerability that came through on camera. If you can elicit a sound bite like that, you will have gone a long way toward producing a memorable story.

Of course, Peterson would not have delivered such a soliloquy if I had cut him off halfway through it.

So many reporters forget to utilize the sound of silence, instead interjecting and hurrying their subjects. The best storytellers get out of the way, allowing their interviewees to express their thoughts.

"As humans, we don't like a gap in the conversation," Pittman points out. "Especially if it's something important, if you let the silence linger, [your interview subject] is gonna say the most profound thing. So let it breathe ... and give them the space to give you the sound bite."

Of course, since you too are human, you will also feel tempted to fill the gaps. You will want to avoid the awkwardness of staring at someone for several seconds as you wait for that brilliant sound bite.

But give it a shot. Heck, try it in normal conversation.

To put a twist on an old expression, if you don't have anything immediate to say, don't say it.

Starting Wide, Then Going in Tight (Photographer Edition)

Throughout the process of conducting an interview, a reporter generally sticks to that above rhythm, starting with wider, broader questions and gradually getting deeper and more revealing.

The same philosophy applies in a visual sense for a photographer – or an MMJ shooting her or his own story.

Pittman personifies this. We already know he begins his interviews with the widest possible question: "Why are we here?" But he also, for that question, frames his interview subjects in the widest possible shot.

"Usually I start wide," he says, waiting until he hears that nice declaratory sound bite that sets the situation. "Then I go ahead and move my shot."

Pittman does this regularly during his interviews, popping for a few questions to a lower angle or zooming to a tighter shot. By the time he wraps up, he has collected numerous angles that all contain several usable sound bites. "It's a good way to keep a mental track of what sound you have. It's like, 'If I have moved [the camera] four times, I'm good here.'"

Pittman has developed a personal routine for shooting one interview from multiple angles. It must surely seem like a lot of work, particularly when solo video journalists should be focusing primarily on their interviews' substance, not their style.

I would recommend incorporating this philosophy in steps. For example, let's say you usually only shoot interviews from one spot with one zoom length. On your next interview, try adding a second look midway through by zooming to a tight shot. Once you master that step, take another one by seeking a second location for your camera. Place it on the ground, perhaps, and shoot part of the interview from a lower angle.

This method requires focus and a great deal of practice, but it pays off in visual variety.

Again, use your solo status to your advantage. You do not need to request anyone's permission to move the camera or change your zoom length. You can streamline the process and pick whichever spots you feel are most appropriate for moving.

In fact, the camera-moving method should work in concert with your questions, to the point where you should aim to use tight shots for more emotional topics. When someone opens his or her heart, you want to capture that person's emotions and expressions as best you can. Tight shots enable you to do this. They also tend to make the background less visible and relevant, focusing a viewer's attention solely on the words and appearance of the person in the frame.

Here, again, is where being a one-person crew enables you to improvise. Want to change your angle and go to a wider shot? Don't do so while asking a particularly emotional question. Want to ask such a question and be able to concentrate on the person's answer? Wait until you have zoomed the camera to a tighter look.

As Pittman says, "You don't want to be that person who, at the most emotional time, is fumbling with the camera. You want to be there in the moment."

But if you keep moving the camera, aren't you reminding your interview subject of that camera, thus increasing the difficulty of eliciting authentic, open sound bites?

"Feel them out," Pittman says. Some people speak more freely than others, and you will likely be able to tell quickly where your particular interview subject falls on that spectrum. "The most important part is getting good sound. That trumps having a fancy shot."

Of course, you can capture numerous angles in a far less awkward setting by conducting the interview while shooting B-roll. I, for one, usually do both: I begin with a more formal sit-down interview and then ask my interview subject to continue to wear a wireless microphone while I shoot footage.

I often rely on that second part to get my most genuine sound.

How often have you found yourself in a normal conversation, recounting to a friend a wild experience, and felt the need to show that friend a photo of what happened? You wanted that person to visually understand the moment, right? You wanted her or him to be in the moment with you as much as possible.

You wanted that person to "get it."

The same idea comes through during active interviews. In my experience, people open up far more when they feel like you "get it." During my story about Engines for Emanuel, I conducted half of Peterson's interview while he cleaned his motorcycle. He seemed less restrained during this part, talking about how he picked up his love for riding from his father. Cleaning his bike gave him something to do while we chatted, perhaps distracting him from the camera.

Pittman produced one of the best stories of his career thanks to a similar interview. He was covering the aftermath of a local tornado, and he drove to a disaster recovery center where dozens of displaced residents had shown up.

Then he spotted Charlene.

"Instead of jumping in and asking an official, I just stood there for a minute and took in the scene," he recalls. "I watched people and read people, and then I decided, 'This woman would be a good person to talk to.'"

She was sitting on a bench, waiting her turn, attempting to make sense of all that had happened.

"She wasn't going anywhere," Pittman says. "I could just go around, and because there was so much going on, that's what gave me so many opportunities."

Charlene quickly proved to be a sound bite machine.

"Where I live, the whole neighborhood was destroyed."
"I mean, this is like a little Katrina going on."
"I don't have nothing. I just have the clothes on my back."
"I'm really, really hurting right now."

(Mrozinski, 2014)

Pittman captured nearly every quote from a different angle, and he edited them in a way that kept the piece moving visually. The story won an NPPA award and remains one of my favorite Pittman packages.

"Everything she said was gold," he recalls. "I started wide, and she said some good stuff, so I got tight. Then I was like, 'I have what I need, so let me just go crazy and see what I can do.' You want to get the important stuff first to tell the story, and once you get that, then you can take more risks."

Handling Interview Adversity

Of course, sometimes you do not receive the blessing of a sound-bite machine. Sometimes you face an interview subject – or an interview situation – that just won't cooperate.

For example, how do you conduct an interview when you are not the only journalist conducting it?

Virtually every media market in America features a newspaper, multiple TV stations, radio stations, bloggers, and digital and independent journalists. I regularly find myself on the same story, and at the same scene, as several other news crews, and I have learned to use my competition to my advantage.

For example, in my never-ending search for unique camera angles, I can move my gear much more easily – and much less awkwardly – while someone else occupies the interview subject with a question.

In the spring of 2015, Tyrone Brooks, a longtime civil rights activist and state representative in Georgia, pleaded guilty and no contest to various charges of fraud – one day after resigning his seat. The following day, I headed out to a press event where Brooks planned to speak to the media.

But he didn't plan to back down.

I arrived first and put my microphone on Brooks for a one-on-one interview. We spoke for roughly ten minutes, with Brooks refusing to admit guilt despite having pleaded so in court.

As I began to wrap up, other crews arrived and jumped in, quickly turning my one-on-one into a four-on-one. They asked questions Brooks had already answered, and I did not want to waste time waiting for everyone else to conclude.

So I took the stealthy route. I gradually slipped away from the proceedings … without taking my wireless microphone back from Brooks.

While the former legislator dealt with a new wave of questions, I posted up from various angles and kept collecting sound bites. Brooks continued to make contentious remarks; I captured them from different spots and later edited them into a quick-cut montage. In the script for my package, I referenced the media scrum and sprinkled in several NAT pops of Brooks' curt responses.

I adjusted on the fly not despite my solo status but because of it.

Sometimes, though, any journalist – solo or otherwise – must roll with interview subjects who don't respond as planned.

The two most recurring personalities who wreak havoc on my interviews? The long talker and the short talker.

Long talkers want to answer every question with a dissertation. They do not understand my time constraints, and they want to seize their moment in the spotlight to unfurl seemingly every thought they possess. I try to avoid interrupting these interviewees, instead choosing to guide them in a forthright manner (e.g. "I want to make sure we have time for everything …" or "I know we have very limited time …").

Some long talkers, by the way, are simple filibusterers – politicians and officials who would rather stall and speak in platitudes than answer specific questions. In these cases, I absolutely feel inclined to interrupt – respectfully, but firmly.

Short talkers do the reverse: they do not possess the gift of gab and instead provide two- to three-word answers to every question. You cannot turn someone like this into a fountain of conversation, but you can adjust your questions to elicit longer answers. Avoid yes-or-no questions; instead, pepper the interviewee with whys and hows, and ask two-part questions that force the person to address multiple points.

You can also let a short talker be a short talker.

"If it's some gruff dairy farmer," Pittman says, "and he's giving two-word answers, put them in the story and roll with it. Don't make fun of him; I'm not saying that. This is who he is. So let him be that."

Most likely, though, you will encounter fewer long talkers and short talkers – and more nervous talkers.

These interview subjects, despite your best intentions to create a genuine, open environment, cannot seem to get over the hurdle of being on television. They clam up rather than speak out, and they seem reluctant to trust an unfamiliar reporter.

In these situations, a wise journalist often chooses to pause the proceedings.

One might decide to address the issue, which as a solo act can be done with more empathy and less embarrassment. I have often stopped my recording and simply asked my interview subject, delicately but directly, "Is everything OK?" The person typically appreciates the question and uses the opportunity to express his or her concerns. After we discuss them, I flip open my camera and continue the interview, usually to more open responses.

Some people don't require a conversation, but time. If you sense that, you can always stop the Q&A and move to a different part of the shoot, such as collecting B-roll or other interviews. The stoppage usually allows the interviewee to breathe and reflect, creating a calmer atmosphere when you return for Round 2.

Above all, this topic boils down to one factor: interpersonal communication.

Earlier in this chapter, I mentioned Boyd Huppert, the KARE-TV feature reporter who has won umpteen Emmy and Murrow awards. I have had the privilege to speak alongside him at journalism conferences, and I am always amazed at how many reporters ask him the same question:

"How do you get people to open up to you like that?"

The answer is an example of human connection at its most basic: Huppert listens, and he genuinely cares about their stories.

In my experience, people can usually tell the difference between real and fake. They can pick out which reporters truly want to hear their perspectives and which ones simply want sound bites. If you interact well with others, both during and surrounding your interview, you will develop a stronger relationship with your subjects and receive more forthright answers. If you interact poorly, you will struggle.

Solo video journalists can potentially lose sight of this because of their many other responsibilities, but they should do whatever possible to stay focused. They should keep their to-do lists and technical checks from seeping too far into their interactions.

After all, the last thing you want is too much ice in your soda.
You want that flavor to pop into a beautiful piece of journalism.

References

David, L. (Writer), Seinfeld, J. (Writer), and Cherones, T. (Director) (1991). "The Phone Message" [Television Series Episode]. In Shapiro/West Productions & Castle Rock Entertainment (Producers), *Seinfeld*. Los Angeles, CA: National Broadcasting Company.

Mrozinski, M. (2014, June 2). "An MMJ Life: Mitch Pittman – The Nuances of an MMJ Interview" [Video File]. Retrieved from www.youtube.com/watch?v=gyUz7LQvByU.

Pearl, M. (2015, September 13). Faith Brings Together Riders of Different Races after Charleston Shooting [Video File]. Retrieved from www.11alive.com/story/news/local/features/2015/09/13/faith-brings-together-riders-different-races-after-charleston-shooting/72220638/.

Pittman, M. (2014, June 2). An MMJ Life: Mitch Pittman (KOMO) – "The Nuances of an MMJ Interview" [Web Log Post]. *TV News Storytellers*. Retrieved from www.tvnewsstorytellers.com/an-mmj-life-mitch-pittman-the-nuances-of-an-mmj-interview/

Recording a Stand-up

7

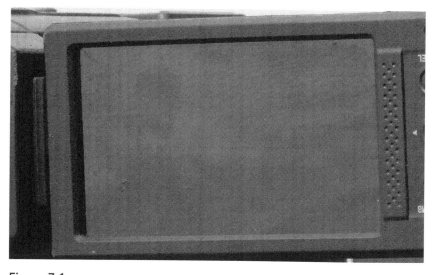

Figure 7.1

Credit: Matt Pearl

The day-to-day deadlines of modern media force journalists to make constant decisions.

Should I get these extra shots? Should I knock on one more door? Should I drive an extra 30 minutes to get one final interview?

These decisions almost always boil down to one fundamental question: *Do I have time?*

If given endless hours and perhaps an endless budget, many of us would surely take whatever steps were needed to fully research, grasp, gather material for, and execute a complete and thorough work of journalism.

Because we do not receive endless hours, we instead regularly perform – either consciously or not – cost-benefit analyses. This is an economic term with a straightforward name; it refers to weighing the benefits of an action ("Getting these shots could make my story more visually interesting …") versus the costs ("but it would probably take another 10 minutes, and I want to leave myself enough time to write and edit …").

We do this on a macro level as well. Many young MMJs, for example, find certain aspects of the job too daunting and labor-intensive (lighting interviews, posting frequently on social media), so they simply decline to learn those skills.

For a long time that was how I felt about shooting my own stand-ups.

I never wanted to get in the way of my stories, so I never put myself in them. I felt limited by stand-ups, thinking they required an excessive amount of time to achieve middling results. Here, I thought, was one area where I could not replicate the work of a traditional crew, so why would I put so much effort into something that would not improve my story?

The cost, in my mind, did not produce the necessary benefit, so I refused to invest.

Then I realized why I should.

In its most standard form, the stand-up seems unnecessary – or, more cynically, like an excuse to put a reporter's face on the screen. Too often it produces the most cliché-ridden caricature of local TV news: an overly dressed reporter, in a far less formal environment, standing perfectly still and speaking with an over-inflected voice into a microphone emblazoned with the station logo.

But when done right, it can benefit a story as much as any video clip or sound bite.

The stand-up enables you to connect with your audience. As a reporter, you serve as a conduit for those watching you, taking them places they cannot go and explaining issues they might not realize or fully grasp.

You can, more frequently than you might think, accomplish this best by putting yourself on camera – but only if you do so in a compelling, engaging, and relatable way.

If you want to see how, go to YouTube and search for a guy whose last name could not be further from his personality.

Joe Little is the I Can't Believe It's Not Butter of solo stand-ups. He consistently produces stand-ups that look like he must have been working with a photographer.

Every January, the veteran reporter for NBC San Diego uploads a video to YouTube that features a montage of a few dozen stand-ups from the previous year. Little's videos leave the rest of us asking two questions:

One: "How did he do that?"

Two: "Why didn't I think of that?"

"I don't look up to MMJs," said the man who has, for most of his career, worked as a solo act. "I look up to photographers and reporters. I want people to think, 'This guy's got a crew of 15 people with him.' I don't want anybody giving me sympathy because I'm an MMJ."

Of course, the people watching Little's work likely do not realize he works alone. That is precisely why, he says, he cannot operate with lowered expectations. Little (Figures 7.2 and 7.3) has always aimed not to match the competition but to outshine it. More often than not, he finds a way to carve a creative path. At his old San Diego station – KGTV – he introduced the concept of multi-shot stand-ups. Soon Little discovered the joys of non-linear editing, and he incorporated various effects to make his stand-ups seem literally impossible. These days Little continues to crank out inventive stand-ups, and he speaks on the topic for companies and

Figure 7.2 Joe Little.

Credit: Matt Pearl

Figure 7.3 Rain, shine, or clouds, a solo stand-up can be done – and look slick.

Credit: Matt Pearl

conferences. He begins each speaking engagement by unveiling his secret weapon: the garden gnome.

"He's an example of what not to do," Little says. "It's the stereotypical reporter stand-up, where you stand in someone's yard with a stick mic doing nothing. I don't care how beautiful or handsome you are; after one second, the viewer's eye is going to leave you and search all around you. I always argue to make it compelling, and the garden gnome is sort of my example: Don't be this guy. Don't waste the viewer's time."

I echo the sentiment. As you read the advice in this chapter, let the garden gnome be your anti-guide.

Let your mind lead the way.

Guidelines and Goals

Perhaps the first step in shooting a powerful stand-up is knowing when not to shoot one.

"I do this montage at the end of the year that has 50 stand-ups in it, but I do 250 stories a year," says Little, "and in at least half of them, I don't make an appearance."

Why not? Because, in those stories, Little would interfere more than he would help.

I typically avoid shooting stand-ups for stories that already possess either strong characters or gripping video. If I cannot enhance – or even sustain – the emotional momentum of a story, I stay out the way. My station also tends to require its reporters to appear on camera to introduce and tag our stories, making stand-ups feel superfluous.

If you plan to insert yourself into a piece, you should understand how your presence would elevate your story.

Says Little: "There's two rules for [when to do] a stand-up: if it helps push the story forward, or if your boss says, 'Do one.'"

I tend to ask myself several additional questions:

- Do I need to spice up the visuals? Will I be able to shoot little else for my story other than static shots of building exteriors? If my B-roll is lacking, a stand-up can stand out.
- Can I demonstrate something? Perhaps I am covering a topic loaded with facts and numbers but little visual representation. I can often convey that information in a memorable way with a well-crafted stand-up.
- Can I walk in the viewer's shoes? Better yet: can I, through a stand-up, enable the viewer to walk in my shoes? This strategy can be effective for serious pieces (like walking through a disaster area) or lighter ones (like going behind the scenes at a major event).

Mostly, I recognize that my presence on camera will also serve as my first visual impression to the audience. I always ask myself, "How can I use my stand-up to connect with the people watching my story?"

"As reporters, we need to identify our voices and tell the viewer, 'This is what this guy looks like,'" says Little, who believes we should treat ourselves the same way we treat our interview subjects. "We would never cover that person forever without establishing who's talking."

We would also never treat our interviewees as our lowest priorities.

"The biggest problem for most people is that the stand-up is an afterthought," Little says. "If you make it an afterthought, it's going to look like an afterthought. I don't wait until the end to think about my stand-ups."

Neither do I. In fact, I usually ask myself the aforementioned questions immediately upon receiving my assignment. If I give myself the green light, I plan the stand-up in advance to flesh out its importance and avoid wasting time in the field.

"I visualize it," says Little. "I think, 'If I do this and this, then I'm going to need to shoot a tight shot here and a cutaway here …'"

I spent a morning shadowing Little as he reported on a dead whale that had washed ashore at Solana Beach, roughly 20 miles north of San Diego. We knew little else when we arrived at a boardwalk overlooking the beach. We stood at a distance from the water but could clearly see the whale, tethered to the shore by a long, thin rope connected to an anchor.

Little immediately got to work.

"Let's take this whale story," he told me. "What are my opportunities to make this a better story at home? The one thing I can't capture [from afar] is that this whale is tied to a rope. But maybe I can stand in front of the lens and point it out."

When Little appeared live 30 minutes later, he did exactly that.

"It adds to the story," he said. "It doesn't detract."

The whole process underscores the importance of pre-planning, even when you have little time. You should brainstorm your story thematically and figure out where a stand-up might fit. You should aim to head out of your newsroom with either a fleshed-out idea or several potential options.

You can do all of this without determining a single line of script.

"You bullet-point it," says Little, who approaches a stand-up like "it's kind of a mini-story in itself: 'Here's this. Here's why.'"

Shooting a Standard Stand-Up

Brainstorming pays off when you arrive on the scene … because you never know how that scene will look.

Far too many times I have envisioned a stand-up in my head before leaving for a shoot, only to adjust that vision after I get there. Sometimes the physical space does not look as I imagined. Other times, the weather gets in the way.

But because I have a general idea of what I want to accomplish, I can focus more in the field on adapting and executing.

"It really is the story that calls for the shot," Little says. "The story dictates the stand-up, not vice versa."

One-person crews, of course, must perform a stand-up without the help of a photographer, which means they must tackle several seemingly daunting obstacles – even when shooting a "garden gnome."

Thankfully, most, if not all, of these obstacles can be conquered with an MMJ's greatest weapons: flexibility and resourcefulness.

"Most of my stand-ups are one shot because I'm trying to live in the moment," says Little, "like if I have two minutes to shoot it while I'm being escorted through a building."

The first challenge: how do you frame yourself without yourself in the shot? Because a news camera cannot shoot a selfie, you must physically set up your camera to face the location of your stand-up … without you in it. Instead, you must use your surroundings, as well as a feature most news cameras do possess.

"The advent of the flip-viewfinder has changed our lives forever," says Little. "I used to shoot something and pray to God I was in frame."

Not anymore. A solo video journalist can now frame a potential shot with some guesswork, flip the viewfinder 180 degrees, and walk into the shot to see if it works.

Of course, you must also ensure you are in focus. In this situation, as with framing, you must rely on whatever else is around.

"I use a lot of things," says Little, "whether it is a light stand or marking something on the ground. There are so many different tricks to shooting a stand-up. If I've got nothing [to focus on], I'll put my keys on the ground."

I always look to the ground. I search for a crack in the sidewalk or any other kind of visible mark, and I focus on that spot before zooming out and framing the camera in the position I desire.

Then, before I press RECORD, I check a mirror.

Here is an area that seems superficial. But if you don't make sure you look presentable, you can submarine a perfectly strong stand-up.

"I see [MMJs] sometimes wearing polo shirts and khaki shorts, or they look like they are the photographer," says Little. "Before I go on camera, I need to look the role."

That means doing your make-up, tucking in your blouse, and straightening your tie. It also means clipping on a lavaliere microphone and checking that its wire does not dangle – and that the mic itself is turned on.

Speaking of microphones, few things restrict the creativity of a stand-up like using a stick microphone instead of a wireless lavaliere. The stick mic typically plugs into the camera with an XLR, which hinders one's ability to move around. Even a wireless stick mic requires a hand to hold it; this limits one's freedom to gesture and demonstrate with both arms.

Little feels more passionately about this topic than anyone I have met. When he posted his 2014 stand-up montage on YouTube, he titled it: "Joe Little 2014 Standups: A Year Without a Stick Mic" (Little, 2015). I think he despises them because they tempt their holders to act like stereotypical reporters: stiff, emotionless, speaking in jargon and fancy words rather than conversational, straightforward language.

His instinct – and mine – is to never be that reporter. When we shoot our stand-ups, we do whatever is possible to communicate it in a relatable, human way.

Take Little's whale story. "You get any rookie or stereotypical reporter out there," he says, "and he'll be like, 'The gray whale beached itself here, and the authorities …' Who's an authority? You're talking to another human. You're not giving a lecture to a science fair. I'm going to just talk. I think, 'How can I relate this best to the viewer at home? How can I tell my buddy at the bar?'"

He will also be active and reference his surroundings, not just telling but showing his audience what he wants them to see.

I cannot overstate the importance of this.

Remember: the stand-up is your one opportunity to show your viewers your face. It is where you enable them to look into your eyes and develop a level of trust and connection.

You don't want to blow it.

You also don't want to leave without checking your work. You cannot, in the field, play back every clip you shoot, but you should always do so with the one clip you cannot physically see while you shoot it. I check both the video and audio in my viewfinder, plugging in headphones to ensure I have recorded my track at the appropriate levels without any outside interference.

This may seem like a superfluous step, but I guarantee it will save your hide.

"I don't leave a scene without checking the audio, making sure I was in focus, and making sure I'm satisfied with the product," Little says.

Why does he do this?

"Because it's me! I take all this time to make sure the person I'm interviewing looks good. Why would I not make that effort for myself?"

Getting Creative

"Effort" is a key word when you decide to turn things up.

Once you learn and practice the above tricks and techniques, you should be able to shoot stationary stand-ups with relative ease.

But you should not stop there.

You should get into what Little calls "mad scientist-type stuff": the stand-ups that grab viewers' attention because they look so different.

Little recalls reporting on a local restaurant that had cooked a feather into one of its chicken nuggets.

"It was awful," he says. "So I put my GoPro – which I love – inside a chicken nugget box, looking up at me. Our job is to take viewers into a place they can never go. Well, I put them in a chicken nugget box!"

Creative stand-ups come in a variety of vehicles. Perhaps they involve, per Little's example, placing a camera in a seemingly impossible spot. Perhaps they contain several shots spliced together as a sequence, similar to how one would shoot B-roll. Perhaps they use creative editing, working with effects to produce something that breaks from reality. (Little once did a story about baseball where he put nine of himself on the field.)

These stand-ups are by definition unique. As a result, neither Little nor I can relay a formula for producing them.

But we can offer a roadmap.

It starts with using your mind – brainstorming and pre-planning like we discussed earlier. Try to first envision your stand-up, and then figure out how to execute it, using the tools you possess as a photographer to make it work.

"It's just thinking about different angles and creative ways," says Little. "I only have one camera and one GoPro. Every situation requires a different thing, but for those crazy ones, I think, 'How can I make it just like my story?' I use NAT pops and really detailed shots. It all goes together. If I have mapped it out in my head, just like with any sequence, it's easy."

MMJs who shoot complex stand-ups often rely, while shooting, on cutaways and sequences. Then, when they edit, they use those shots to establish a seemingly continuous line.

Let's say, for example, you are doing a story that involves a document, and you want to reference it in your stand-up. You can hold the document throughout and use it as a cutaway to create a relatively simple three-shot sequence:

1) WIDE SHOT of you on camera at the scene
2) TIGHT SHOT of the document as you reference it ("So they filed this lawsuit ...")
3) MEDIUM SHOT of you on camera at the scene.

Just like that, you have defeated the specter of the garden gnome.

"I have to edit in my head," says Little about how he approaches such a shoot. "I think, 'I have to go from a long shot to a medium shot ... no, no, no, I've got to go from a long shot to a tight shot to a medium shot.'"

When Little sits down hours later at his laptop, he can edit his stand-up with relative ease.

Some stand-ups, of course, rely largely on creative editing. I will talk far more about editing in Chapter 9 but for now I encourage you to get familiar with the power of your editing software. It can do much more than you think.

Mostly, I implore you to take seriously the concept of the stand-up. Make it worth your time.

"There's no formula for doing a stand-up," says Little, the man who always seems to find new ways to do them. "But if it's something that adds value to the story, then it works. If you are doing it just to be on camera, then you're doing it for the wrong reasons."

"Aim to do better."

Reference

Little, J. (2015, January 4). "Joe Little 2014 Standups: A Year Without a Stick Mic" [Video File]. Retrieved from www.youtube.com/watch?v=ZhpELIbstCs

Career Chronicles

Solo as a Springboard

Few, if any, stories this century received as much attention – or fueled as widespread a ripple – as the 2014 death of Michael Brown in Ferguson, Mo.

The teenager, black and unarmed, was fatally shot by a white police officer. Brown's grandmother, who was expecting him to visit, found his body in the middle of the street. Protests began almost immediately and escalated over several weeks, consuming Ferguson and dominating American media. Hundreds of reporters descended on a town of 20,000, documenting the action and amplifying an important and ongoing conversation about the relationship between black Americans and officers of the law.

Among those hundreds, two journalists in their 20s arrived for the biggest assignments of their careers, prepared to work alone.

Blayne Alexander had developed as an MMJ the traditional way. She began her on-air career in Market #115, grinding in the east Georgia heat in the city of Augusta. Within two years, she had built a reel impressive enough to get noticed two hours west. When managers at WXIA-TV in Atlanta sought a rising star to join their growing roster of solo video journalists, they found a match in a 24-year-old with endless energy and passion. That was in 2011. Three years later, she had established herself so firmly – at both WXIA and then-parent company Gannett – that she received the call to head to Ferguson and join a select group of storytellers to produce reports for Gannett-owned stations nationwide. Alexander loaded her gear and got on a plane.

Emily Kassie had never cared about broadcast news. Her goal was impact. At age 13 she shot her first documentary – a spotlight on gay teens in religious high schools that screened at film festivals in her home city of

Toronto. In college she spent her summers in eastern Africa, convincing her then-boyfriend to assist on a project called *I Married My Gunman's Killer* about intermarriage after the Rwandan genocide. That film would win a Student Academy Award for Documentary. Months before its release, Kassie took her first job out of school: a multimedia journalist position with Huffington Post. One month in, she flew to Ferguson.

Alexander and Kassie took different paths, but each rose quickly, largely by working alone. Each has since continued to rise. Alexander works as a correspondent for NBC News. Kassie is the Director of Visual Projects at the Marshall Project. Neither works as a solo video journalist anymore. But both credit doing it all – and doing it with purpose – for catalyzing their climb.

Many young journalists scoff at the solo life. Perhaps they only want to report, not waste time learning the foundations of shooting and editing. Perhaps they simply find it all too daunting. Perhaps they don't mind the concept but don't want to make a career of it.

They don't need to. In recent years the journalism industry – particularly in video – has grown tentacles from TV stations to digital outlets to documentary houses. Few journalists feel beholden to a specified career track, mainly because the tracks keep changing as the field evolves. Some solo video journalists see no need to part ways with their cameras. Others embrace the job – and the many skills it develops – and propel themselves to positions where working alone is no longer a necessity.

I was working alongside Alexander (Figure CC2.1) when she recognized her time to pivot.

In 2016, she and I flew to Rio as part of a 25-person team from TEGNA to cover the Summer Olympics. We split the duties for our station in Atlanta, turning two to three packages each per day and following dozens of Georgia athletes as they aimed for medals. We worked alongside each other for three weeks, coordinating everything from travel to story schedule.

But when we produced stories, we worked mostly alone.

"Going to Rio, honestly, was like the pinnacle of MMJ-ness," Alexander told me three years later. "I had never worked that hard for three weeks straight. It was emotionally taxing. It was physically taxing. I felt so much stronger as a journalist, reporter, and person after that experience."

Because she had reached the pinnacle, she knew she was ready to look beyond.

Within six months, Alexander learned of an opening for NBC News Channel's Washington correspondent. She applied. She got the job. She moved to the network. Two years later, she received a new title: correspondent for NBC News. These days she turns stories with a photographer, audio operator,

Figure CC2.1 Blayne Alexander.

Credit: Cliff Robinson

editor, and multiple producers. In her first month, Alexander flew to London to cover the rise of teenage tennis star Coco Gauff at Wimbledon. Her reports resembled the kinds of pieces she had produced in Rio. But this time, she worked with a team.

When I watch Alexander's stories, I notice similarities between her network assignments and the subjects she covered at WXIA. A year before the Olympics, she drove to Alabama to spotlight the 50th anniversary of the civil rights march from Selma to Montgomery. One month after our return from Rio, Alexander hit the road again to report from Washington on the soon-to-open National Museum of African American History and Culture.

She received each of these assignments, including the 2016 Summer Games, because of her solo status – and because she knew how to leverage that status to her greatest advantage.

"I always pitched myself as an MMJ," Alexander said. Often she pitched herself as, let's say, an MMJ+. With Selma, for example, "they had already decided to send an anchor. I remember wandering into our EP's office like, 'Hey! If I go, you know I can shoot pieces. And if you send a photographer with me, we can churn out double the stories.'"

Many of those stories ended up on the reel that got her to NBC.

Alexander's success reflects many factors, from her thoughtfulness in reporting to her commitment to connecting with others. But she also embraced her role as a soloist, even if she didn't plan on owning that role forever. In Augusta, she competed with three reporters at her station in a running competition called the Stand-up Standoff. On a given day, they would go on their assignments and see who came back with the most creative stand-up, a distinction voted on by their newsroom colleagues. Of the four, Alexander was the only MMJ.

"Half the people there didn't want to MMJ," she says of her first job. "They were like, 'I'm just trying to get to Philly, and then I'll have a photographer.' And their work looked like crap! The product is kind of your calling card. You can't just say, 'I know eventually I'm going to be an anchor on the Today Show and I'm never going to have to shoot.' Nobody's going to see past that if they're just seeing bland shots. If the package and presentation don't look good, you're not going to get very far."

Alexander focused on her craft, but she didn't forget her larger goals. I had been at WXIA for a year when she took the cubicle behind me, and I immediately noticed her ambition and awareness to produce stories with lasting value. She pitched trips like Selma and DC because she understood the stories she wanted to cover. Solo video journalists – heck, most journalists, period – get thrown into the daily mix and rarely receive chances to lift their heads. Alexander proved her worth as a reliable reporter, then capitalized on that clout to seek stories with meaning.

"You have to identify those stories that remind you why you started this journey in the first place," she advises. "If you like stories about dogs, great! Find those dog stories. If you enjoy sending FOIA requests and digging into people's tax dollars, do that. Don't just let the assignments happen to you, because that's when you'll burn out. You have to find the why in what you do."

Alexander knew her "why" and recognized stories that would feed it. Then she offered options for her coverage that made sense to all ... not unlike another journalist who shined first as a soloist and now holds a far more expansive title.

Before she flew to Ferguson, before she won a Student Academy Award, before she produced her first documentary at 13, Emily Kassie (Figure CC2.2) found herself at an early fork that presaged her desires as a storyteller.

She was in first grade. Her class was producing a project about the Wetlands. Everyone wanted to make a report about otters ... except her.

"I was just really determined to do swans," Kassie says. "But no one else wanted to do a report on swans, so I just did it by myself. I was the only one in the class who did my own project and didn't collaborate."

Figure CC2.2 Emily Kassie.

Credit: Leslye Davis

On the Wetlands project, she worked alone. And when I first learned of Kassie nearly two decades later, it was for a different solo project: a piece called "Hunting for Addicts" about a health care scam in Palm Beach County that won the NPPA's Best of Photojournalism Award for Solo Video Journalism In-Depth. I was stunned by her storytelling maturity. Everything – the camerawork, the lighting, the pacing, and the flair – seemed masterful. I couldn't believe I hadn't heard of her. I couldn't believe someone in her mid-20s had carved out such a unique lane, freelancing for the New York Times and NBC Left Field. I couldn't believe she had carved it alone.

I later learned she hadn't. Kassie worked by herself on "Hunting for Addicts," but, I discovered, she often collaborated. The same year she won the NPPA award for her solo work, she won a separate NPPA award for Team Video Journalism. Kassie, I learned, did it all when necessary but preferred to join forces when possible.

She still operates that way. As a director at the Marshall Project, Kassie engineers collaborations with other news and film organizations, like The Guardian and Sundance Institute. She oversees ambitious productions about the US criminal justice system, and she often performs many of the tasks of a solo video journalist. But she rarely does them all at once, and she rarely works alone.

"I usually try to work with [directors of photography] whenever I can now," Kassie says, "and have a two-camera shoot so I'm not on my own. But

I'm still doing a lot of the shooting, editing, producing and directing alone. It depends on the project and what we've rationed for. When I have a choice, I choose to collaborate."

Perhaps because Kassie never went through the broadcast pipeline, where traditional reporters and solo video journalists are often placed into sparring categories, she never became indoctrinated with the concept of distinct newsroom positions. She simply did what she could with who was available, and she never scoffed at doing it all. "Working alone was more of a necessity because of budget," she says of her early-career work. "What was available to me at the time was myself and my camera, so I had to see what lemonade I could make. And some of that lemonade was sour."

Much like Alexander, Kassie understood her deeper ambitions. As a result, she never held back from attempting and offering stories that might seem too daunting for one person. One month after she arrived at the Huffington Post, she pitched herself for Ferguson. When the web site unveiled Highline, its long-form concept embracing magazine-style journalism and multimedia presentation, she sought its new managers and, she says, "hitched myself to their truck."

She also never stopped seeking inspiration – and people to provide it.

"As much as I loved the idea of being a one-woman show," she says, "eventually I graduated to thinking, 'I just want to work with people who are more talented than me.' Any chance I could get, I'd take."

That mindset propelled Kassie, both as a staffer with the Huffington Post and as a freelancer securing assignments across the digital landscape. By striving as a soloist, she says, she developed an overall understanding of every link of the storytelling chain. She became an ideal manager. When leaders at the Marshall Project targeted her to oversee visual projects, Kassie says it was the first time an outlet had pursued her instead of her pursuing the outlet.

"You have to develop tenacity and patience when you're working alone," she says, "just to be able to persist and push through things. That kind of resolve is essential to getting things done. You have to have a ton of initiative.

"I think my entire career has been about initiative."

You might find it strange that the person whose words you're reading – the person who wrote a book about solo video journalism and even titled it *The Solo Video Journalist* – would understand and even advocate a career path that doesn't include working alone.

But I have never consumed myself with titles. I preach passions. I believe in the power of working alone to fulfill those passions, but I mostly I believe in fulfilling them however possible. When I produce documentaries, I partner with a graphic editor and digital producer. On rare occasions, I ask for an additional photographer. I seek critiques from my colleagues, and I welcome collaboration. I lead with ambition.

Alexander and Kassie share that DNA. They both ended up in Ferguson because they had already established newsroom reputations as impactful storytellers. They held the confidence of their bosses to understand, investigate, and find nuance in the larger issues looming over Michael Brown's death. On that week in 2014, each journalist arrived in Ferguson ready to report – and to do so alone.

In that instance, neither needed to.

Managers at Gannett saw too many safety risks and paired every reporter, including Alexander, with a photographer. Kassie occasionally branched off on her own, but mostly she teamed with the Huffington Post's print reporters and provided a video treatment of important stories. Both invested their work with the passion and purpose that guides them today, solo or otherwise. Both made their bosses proud.

Both continue to shine.

Part III

Putting It Together

Logging and Writing   **8**

Figure 8.1

Credit: Matt Pearl

Roughly a year into my first job in local TV news, I sat in front of my computer one night facing a journalist's two worst enemies:

A blank screen and a looming deadline.

But the screen was not in my newsroom, and the deadline was not for a newscast. I was sitting at home, staring with bloodshot eyes at the computer in my bedroom. My deadline? The clock had just struck midnight, and I needed to, at some point, go to sleep.

But I couldn't yet ... not when I had just received the burst of inspiration that would affect the way I did my job from that moment forward.

At the time, I had been struggling professionally. As a one-man sports department in Sioux City, Iowa, I spent my weekdays producing, shooting, writing, editing, and anchoring two sportscasts a night. To be sure, I enjoyed it. I had always dreamed of becoming a sports anchor and reporter, and now someone was actually paying me to do it.

But I battled stress the whole time. I grappled with the undeniable culture shock of moving to a "big city" the size of my suburban hometown. I worked grueling and intense hours, often self-prescribed, in my efforts to tell great stories and improve my skills.

I had begun to think those skills had plateaued. I felt hungry to get better but helpless as to how. I struggled to find any examples around me whose work pushed me forward. This was 2004, before reporters and stations shared stories on web sites, Facebook, and Twitter.

One night in November, I found inspiration in a three-year-old article from a two-year-old book.

I cracked open the 2002 edition of the *Best American Sports Writing* anthology, which chronicles the year's finest sports journalism. I had read it before, but on this night, I circled back and reread its opening piece: a feature by Los Angeles Times writer Bill Plaschke titled "Her Blue Haven."

It was beautiful. Plaschke detailed his correspondence with an LA Dodgers blogger living with cerebral palsy. The blogger, Sarah Morris, wrote with a head pointer because she could not control her fingers.

I found myself enthralled with Plaschke's craft. I envied his inventiveness, thoughtfulness, and refusal to waste a word. I appreciated his talent for conveying emotion and context while crafting a multi-layered narrative. Mostly, I admired his ability to tell a touching, genuine story in a completely original way.

I put down the book and, instead of going to sleep, walked over to my computer and sat down. I opened a new document, stared at a blank screen, and prepared to write Plaschke a thank-you note.

Why? His work had illuminated a truth I have followed ever since:

More than anything else, great storytelling comes down to great writing. It's as simple as that.

Writing is the most universal thing we do in journalism. Not everyone regularly picks up a camera. Not everyone edits videos. But everyone writes – from e-mails to texts to Post-it notes to checklists to recipes to documents to diaries. People write more today than at any time in human history, which makes our evolution as writers fascinating. Author Clive Thompson, who has scribed hundreds of articles and several books about how we communicate, summed it up beautifully in a post for the social blog site Medium:

> These days, people write insanely more text than they did before the Internet and mobile phones came along. So the volume of experimentation is correspondingly massive and, for me, delightful. One joy of our age is watching wordplay evolve at the pace of E. coli.
>
> (Thompson, 2015)

How does this apply to solo video journalists? It informs everything we do. Writing is the bedrock of virtually every form of media, and those who develop that foundation will be far more prepared for however the landscape changes.

Here is how one current one-person outfit – and award-winning writer – described it to me:

"Good writing exists everywhere. It exists in an iPhone video you shoot for Facebook. It exists in your web story. It's everything we do."

"It can make people cringe and make people cry."

Many modern-day TV news journalists enter the business as do-it-all reporters, patiently eyeing the day when they can drop the "do-it-all" and simply be reporters.

Ted Land (Figure 8.2) went the opposite route.

He entered the business in 2007 and held virtually every job in TV before realizing he most desired the title of MMJ.

"I didn't feel complete just being behind the camera shooting the story, although I loved that," he says of a brief stint as a photographer in Chicago, which came after a year of producing and anchoring weekend newscasts in Reno. "It was a fun job, but I always felt the need of 'Give me the pen. I'd like to write the story. I think I can do it better.'"

Land spent four years in Anchorage, Alaska and then took an MMJ job in South Bend, Ind. One year later, he captured a Chicago/Midwest Emmy for Solo Video Journalism.

He soon received an even greater honor: the National Edward R. Murrow Award ... for writing.

Competing against traditional reporters around the country, Land won one of the industry's most coveted prizes, and he did so as a solo act. Land now works at one of the nation's premier storytelling stations, KING-TV in Seattle, and sees himself as an "MMJ for life."

Figure 8.2 Ted Land.

Credit: Marlowe Ramirez

"It's very empowering to think that, as a multimedia journalist, you can still write meaningful and memorable stories," he says. "I'm really proud that I didn't have to sacrifice anything to do this all by myself. My advice to younger MMJs is to take the writing very seriously and make it matter, because that is what will make you stand out."

As Land and any other successful reporter will you, serious writing begins long before you place your fingers on the keyboard.

Writing before You Start Writing

By now, this point probably sounds obvious, but it is worth repeating:

The best storytellers in general – but specifically the best solo video journalists – think about every step of the process during every step of the process.

When conducting an interview, they think about how a person's responses might fit into their overall story. When shooting sequences, they think about how those sequences will be edited hours later.

And during each individual step in gathering material for a story, the best one-person crews ponder how they will ultimately write it.

This is partly a function of time – as in, not having enough. Writers are often romanticized as independent spirits who can labor over every line, await a burst of inspiration, and operate outside the bounds of limits and deadlines. In reality, journalists receive no such leeway. Most of us get seven to eight hours, if that, to produce a story from start to finish. The typical reporter probably allots 30–40 minutes to physically write.

Such a schedule offers little room to showcase one's inner Hemingway.

Another constraint? The need to match words to video. Print or online reporters can operate without considering a story's accompanying visuals; they can, and must, focus on structuring sentences to fit how people read. Television reporters must write for how people hear, creating lines of script that work in concert with their edited video. Boring, non-matching video can submarine even the best-written TV story. Exciting, matching video? That can elevate one's writing.

In fact, many perceived constraints can actually become advantages for television reporters, particularly those who do it all.

"I think being an MMJ has enhanced my writing," says Land, "because it's a much more organic product. It's my doing. It's my creation. There's no question about what the visuals will be. And if you know what they are, you'll be able to write a better story."

The best way to jump-start your writing in the field is to think thematically about your story. In other words, you should constantly ask yourself a simple question: "Why is this important?"

The logic here is simple: if you know why your story matters, you will best be able to convey its importance to your viewers.

Few stories in 2015 mattered more to Atlanta football fans than the development of the Falcons' new stadium. The team had embarked on the project several years earlier, with the blessing of $200 million from city taxpayers. But that money came with conditions, mainly that the Falcons' owners would devote some of it to developing the nearby Westside neighborhood. A quarter-century earlier, the team and city built the Falcons' previous stadium, the Georgia Dome, with similar promises of Westside revitalization. Those promises had mostly proven empty, leaving both residents and officials wary of a repeat performance.

That spring, I received an assignment to check on the progress – not of the stadium, whose overall cost had jumped to a whopping $1.5 billion, but of the Westside. As I thought about the story, I knew I would want to speak to Westside residents to get a better sense of their outlook. But I did not know where to find them.

So I drove around, spending roughly half an hour in the car observing the surroundings. I could not say what I expected to find, but I at least understood the story's significance in that area: residents wanted respect and acknowledgment from city leaders who had, they felt, too often ignored them.

Then I found what I did not know I was looking for.

As I drove along the neighborhood's main drag, I saw a giant chalkboard facing the road. In the top left corner, an artist had painted the words:

"I Dream To One Day ..."

The artist had also left chalk at the board's base, so residents and passersby could fill in their dreams on the otherwise blank canvas.

Many had done just that. I observed a chalkboard crammed with the most diverse set of dreams I could imagine (see Figure 8.3). I shot some footage and then walked next door to a barbershop, where I interviewed a barber and longtime Westside resident, Steve Judy. When I asked Steve if he knew about the chalkboard, he responded, "I pass it every day! I just see people putting their hopes up there. When you read the most serious ones, they'll get you to thinking."

Then he said the sentence that brought everything together:

"But most of the time, the weather washes it away."

As soon as I heard that line, I knew it would become the centerpiece of my story. I could not have pictured a better metaphor for the neighborhood itself.

"For so long," I would later write, "the promises to revive this struggling side of town have also washed away ... promises born again with the nearby construction of the Falcons' new stadium" (Pearl, 2015).

Figure 8.3 This chalkboard became a defining feature on Atlanta's Westside.
Credit: Matt Pearl

In that moment with Steve Judy, I had not yet formulated my words. I had simply found my theme – my way to eloquently answer the question, "Why is this important?"

This anecdote illustrates another constructive way I use my information gathering to enhance my writing: I start to put together the puzzle. When I observe a moment like Steve Judy's chalkboard comment, I immediately brainstorm how to fit it into my script. Will it work best at the beginning of my story? Will it make a greater impact towards the end? How does it fit into the overall narrative? Great stories often hinge on powerful moments, and a great storyteller stays on the lookout for them.

Land keeps a mental checklist of those moments. During interviews, he says, "I listen for sound that matters, and if I'm not getting it, I generally carry the conversation a little longer."

I rarely write actual lines of script while I work in the field. I instead try to prioritize shooting and interviewing, thinking about the story's overall framework rather than specific sentences. But I use my phone to occasionally jot down a nifty turn of phrase, and I use my drive time to think aloud about my opening and closing lines. These are usually the toughest and most crucial sections to write, for reasons we will explore later. If I can jump-start that process, even if I cannot physically write anything down, I will make my job much easier when I get back to the station and sit down at my desk.

Then I begin the next part of the process – a step that, when done right, dramatically improves my script and my story.

Logging Interviews and Video

When I first met with Land to discuss this chapter, I started by asking about his strategies for logging, or the act of transcribing interviews and B-roll in preparation for writing.

His response? "Logging is actually pretty minimal for me."

It was a fascinating answer ... because it completely betrays the amount of focus and attention Land gives to this important step. Every time we spoke about writing in general, Land talked more about logging than any other task. He regularly touted the marked increase in quality that comes from transcribing as many details and sound bites as possible.

So why, for Land, is logging so minimal?

Because he rarely has enough time to do it.

Logging may be the most collapsible step in an MMJ's entire day. It usually arrives just as the hours start ticking away before one's deadline, and it often seems like the easiest task to slim down.

"Generally when I get back from a story, I have a pretty good idea of what I've shot," Land says. "That's the beauty of being an MMJ: you don't have to log as much as you thought. There are times when it's breaking news and you just skip logging altogether, because you know what you have. For a big feature, you can log everything, and then you have a nice little packet of all of your sound. But [normally] the reality is, you just don't have time for that."

For the next few paragraphs, let's pretend we do.

As a one-person crew facing a looming deadline, you will always feel tempted to take shortcuts. Sometimes, as Land points out, you must. But you should approach your day with the intent to log as much as possible, because it will absolutely elevate your writing.

If nothing else, you should log your interviews with thoroughness and detail. When you do so, you essentially write part of your script, where your own lines will weave in and out of the words of your interview subjects. In a business where every word counts, you want to avoid duplicating the content of your sound bites.

At his desk in Seattle, Land showed me an example where minimal logging came back to hurt him. He played a story about recent flooding in the city of Aberdeen, where he described the efforts of neighbors and volunteers to clean up affected homes. At one point in the piece, Land used the phrase "soaked drywall" and then cut to a volunteer holding such drywall and saying, "Soaked and wet at the bottom" (Land, 2015).

Land paused the story, laughed, and shook his head. He had repeated the word "soaked."

"Had I logged that," he said, "I would have written something a little more thoughtful."

Land, I thought, was being hard on himself. I had barely noticed the repetition before he pointed it out. But his minor "mistake" often occurs on a larger, more obvious scale. For example, perhaps you have seen a story with a section like this:

> Reporter: Smith was arrested last night but told reporters he didn't do it.
> Smith: "I didn't do it!"

The reporter here could have easily eliminated the second part of his track and saved several seconds for additional details or moments. This is why you should get in the habit of logging sound bites verbatim, not paraphrased. You need to know your interviewee's words so you can more effectively write around them.

You also want to remember how they sounded and looked. Don't just listen. Watch your interviews. As Land says, "Their expressions say just as much as the words. So I'm always looking out for those kinds of things."

His story about flooding showed me a textbook example of why he does.

About 70 seconds into his 100-second piece, Land presented a sound bite where one of the volunteers, Jim, explained what the experience meant to him.

"You know what?" said Jim. "Helping these people out is more important to me than anything in life." He then paused, straightened up his body, and turned his gaze from the drywall to Land's eyes: "Including the Super Bowl!"

As he said that last line, Jim raised his eyebrows and added a teeth-filled smile that brought it all home. He had been presented until that point as a stoic, get-down-to-business type. Through one line, Land showed Jim's humor and heart.

It's a great moment – the kind you want to pick out when logging, so you can remember later to write to it.

Jim's Super Bowl quote emphasizes another tactic: log for emotion, not information. A journalist's first priority, of course, is to get the facts right. When I write my story, I tend to use my track to paraphrase its information. I find I can summarize a story's facts more quickly than the people I interview, largely because I can write those facts beforehand instead of reciting them on the spot. But when re-watching and logging an interview, I always search for the sentences that convey a person's feelings. I seek sound bites that are short and powerful; I rarely run a quote longer than ten seconds, reserving those moments for the most raw and poignant displays of emotion.

(You'll note this parallels the best practices for conducting interviews. Again, each step of the process informs the others.)

The best storytellers, I feel, find the time to log everything, not just the interview. They understand that knowing their B-roll better enables them to write to it. When I transcribe my footage for longer stories and documentaries, I log virtually every shot. I preface each one with a WS, MS, or TS to define its role in the sequence ("WS" = wide shot, "MS" = medium shot, "TS" = tight shot). I use shorthand terms that speed up the process, even if only I can comprehend them. I often log five to six pages worth of details – enough to temporarily overwhelm me.

How long does it take? I can usually log in real time, so if I shoot 90 minutes of video, I will need 90 minutes to transcribe it. On a day-to-day basis, I must be more judicious with my time, and I rarely shoot so much video that I lose track of what I have. This lessens the impulse to log every shot, but I still try to scan all of it. Doing so jogs my memory about specific moments that might fit into the story. I scrawl down highlights, including opportunities for natural sound. When the time comes, I write them into my script.

Land does this too. "If you were to look at my logs," he says, "you would see certain things in bold or with an asterisk next to it." He specifically targets the critical moments that will shape his piece: "How many great little moments do you capture each day in a story? Maybe three or four, if you're lucky? That's not a lot to write down."

As I listened to the recording of my interview with Land, I could not help but think back to one of the greatest quotes I have heard regarding TV news. I was interning at News 12 New Jersey, shadowing a sports anchor as he logged video for a package. I watched him take furious notes and study the facial expressions of his interviewees. I asked the anchor if he always put this much care into a seemingly less consequential part of the job.

The anchor said he could not always log with such meticulousness. The time constraints of the job, he said, prevented it.

Then he turned to me, raised his index finger, and grew a wry smile.

"But," he said, "when I have the time … every time."

He said those last two words with the joy of someone who loves to tell stories, who loves to immerse himself in the minutiae of his video because he knows it will create a better product. His statement continues to drive me, nearly two decades later, when I think about logging.

When I have the time to do it right, I indeed do it every time … and it always helps.

Following Your Path

Then, after spending all day setting the table, it's time to dine.

Writing is where all of one's preparation and advance work begins to pay off. It can be one of the most arduous, frustrating tasks, laden with the temptations of clichés, stereotypes, bland language, and overall milquetoast execution.

But it can also be liberating: an opportunity to craft words and sentences in a singular way; a chance to determine what information gets broadcast and what doesn't; a moment to turn all of one's brainstorming into an actual, tangible story.

On a typical day, it takes about 30 minutes.

"I don't need that much time," says Land, "and if you give me hours, I'm just going to do something else. Writing to me is creative. It's important.

But it's also a task, and it needs to be done. So you get it done, and you move on."

For a solo video journalist, this mindset is essential. A traditional reporter can write a script and then turn it over to a photographer to edit the final video. As a do-it-all reporter, you are your own editor. If you take too long to write your story, you create more pressure for yourself during the edit.

This is why I harp on the importance of time management and advance planning. When I actually sit down to put words on paper (or, more likely, the screen of my computer or cell phone), I obey many of the same principles I have followed throughout my day, including some mentioned earlier in this chapter.

First, I think about why the story matters. Ideally, I have focused on this question during each step of the gathering process. I specifically consider it here, when I can smell the coming deadline and often feel stumped about how to fit my many great details and sound bites into a 90-second package. By refocusing my mind on what makes the story important, I gain a sense of clarity that dictates how I frame my script.

Second, I focus on my first and last lines. The *Best American Sports Writing* book that featured "Her Blue Haven" also featured an introduction from Rick Reilly, the famed columnist, in which he offers ten tips for great writing.

Tip #2? "Get 'em in the tent."

Reilly drills the importance of a strong lead. Without one, he says, "they'll never appreciate your death-defying twinkle-toe transition in the twenty-third paragraph" (Reilly, 2002). Same goes for TV. Your introductory line of script combines with your first sound bite or NAT pop to set the tone and theme for your story.

Your closing line is equally important. Land lives by the advice of another writing legend, KARE-TV reporter Boyd Huppert, who needs a wheelbarrow every year to carry out his Emmys. "A good closing line," Land recounts Huppert saying, "should make you say, 'Ain't that the truth?'"

Finding such a line can become a creative challenge, especially under the pressure of a deadline. But, Land says, once he uncovers it, the rest of his writing "takes about five minutes."

Then, think about your video. Here is where I look back at my log and mine it for inspiration. How can I write to certain shots? What sequences match specific lines of script? I cannot count how many times I have been stuck on how to write a certain line and found the answer by scanning my log.

Mainly, I think about structure. I have spent the day amassing material, but I must now determine how to arrange it to engage my audience.

I achieve the most success when I use a narrative structure. This is an imprecise concept that differs for each story, but it typically involves a rhythm and flow that resembles a short film or book chapter:

- Grab the audience's attention by getting 'em in the tent.
- Once they are in the tent, flesh out your story in a way that builds interest and steadily unveils new information.
- Reveal the biggest or deepest moment for maximum impact (the climax of your story).
- Sum it up with a strong finish (see Huppert's idea of, "Ain't that the truth?").

Within this structure, I remind myself how everything I write is connected. I aim to arrange my first line in a way that sets up the next line, and I try to unfold my story's themes and moments in a substantive order.

This keeps my story from feeling like a report.

Later, in Chapter 11, you will hear from Huppert himself about what separates a story from a report. In my mind, the differences lie in the dimensions. A report consists of a flat reading of facts and possesses little narrative flow, while a story contains layers of subtexts, visuals, and characters.

A report is often unmemorable. A well-told story is unforgettable.

Making It Count

The following is a script for a story of mine, titled "Cabbagetown Christmas Miracle," that received an NPPA award for deadline reporting. (For clarity, I have put my reporter track in italics.)

As you read the script, count the number of factual statements:

(NAT pop: street noise)
Brad: "Cabbagetown is a small town in the middle of the city."
And in the heart of Atlanta …
Brad (talking to customer): "You want that for here or to go?"
Brad Kunard has seen his small town rise up …
Brad (talking to customer): "We thought we were gonna close."
Customer (talking to Brad): "What?"
Brad (talking to customer): "Yeah …"
… Rescuing his Cabbagetown business, Little's Food Store.
Brad: "It feels like a Cabbagetown Christmas miracle."

A miracle for someone who has seen this story before, in far more tragic terms.
(NAT pop: rain)
Ten years and four months ago, a 70-foot oak tree crushed Brad's moving vehicle, with his wife and two children inside. They died instantly.
Brad: "At your lowest point, to see people rally around and want to make sure you're OK and that you do OK, it touches you in such a real way."
And years later, when Brad felt himself shrinking again …
(NAT pop: wrapper)
Along …
Brad (talking to customer): "Hi, this is me; my name is Brad …"
Came Little's …
Customer (talking to Brad): "How ya doing?"
Brad took over the classic Cabbagetown building and turned it into an eclectic grocery and grill. But last week …
Brad (reading a Facebook post off his phone): "Little's is closing at the end of December …"
Long overdue repairs and far too high a cost forced Brad to call it quits. His community said, "No."
Customer (talking to Brad): "Have a good night …"
Within a week, Brad's Cabbagetown neighbors raised enough money so that, on this night, Brad can now tell his customers this:
Brad (talking to customer): "We'll get this place restocked."
Brad (talking to customer; different shot): "We're gonna get the store open."
Brad (talking to customer; a third shot): "This will be enough to keep me going."
He calls it a Christmas miracle. But mostly, Brad calls this another example, in the big city, of small-town community.
Brad: "That support means everything, and I love the fact that people in Atlanta are that way."
In Cabbagetown, Matt Pearl, 11Alive News.

(Pearl, 2013)

This is an uplifting news story that does not necessarily feel like hard news. Even so, in my track alone, I counted more than two dozen factual statements.

Before I put those statements on the air, I confirmed every last one – from the size of Cabbagetown to the height of the oak tree.

Regardless of the story, the facts always come first. They indicate your credibility as a journalist, and they dictate the baseline of trust you receive from your audience. I reread and examine every sentence to ensure I get them right, and I take the blame if I get one wrong. A producer or manager may read my script for approval, but as the reporter I possess the most knowledge of my story's details. If I fail to spot a mistake, I cannot depend on anyone else to catch it.

I also try to avoid making statements of assertion unless I absolutely earn them. For example, take this line from the above script:

> *He calls it a Christmas miracle. But mostly, Brad calls this another example, in the big city, of small-town community.*

This was my closing line, and I used it to connect Brad's individual story to the larger theme of community. But I could not have written that line if (a) Brad had not either said or indicated it, or (b) it did not fully reflect what my viewer had seen to that point.

Land describes it like this: "Sometimes you can go out on a limb and make some philosophical statements about life … and it feels good, and that's what a lot of people consider to be 'good writing.' But you can't exaggerate it. There's a fine line between resonating with people and just sounding silly, patronizing people, or lecturing them … because what do you know?"

Writing is, at its heart, a creative tool. But as you fill your script with an array of structural and grammatical flourishes, you should only do so in the service of your story. If you call attention to yourself, rather than your subject, you are doing it wrong.

One way to do it right? Let your sound bites do the talking.

During the section on logging, I spoke of the importance of seeking sound bites that capture emotion, not information. Here is where that philosophy comes around. In my script above, I provide most of the facts. I allow Brad to express his feelings. I could never convey the personal heartache that Brad displays with this quote:

> At your lowest point, to see people rally around and want to make sure you're OK and that you do OK, it touches you in such a real way.

Why would I ever try to duplicate that?

Ultimately, the secret to many stories is to find the moments, then connect the dots. Throughout the whole day, you have been mining for moments. You should structure your script in a way that sets up and earns them.

"Those are the things you want your viewers to see and hear more than anything else," Land says. "You just have to package them in a way that makes sense."

With this story, I did not immediately reveal how the community raised the necessary money to save Brad's store. I first established some valuable foundations:

- Cabbagetown possesses a small-town vibe in a big city.
- The community had come to Brad's rescue a decade earlier, at his lowest point.
- Brad's store held special personal value because of how it helped him recover.
- The store had, in a short time, become an eclectic community favorite.

Then, 75 seconds into the story, I presented the payoff: Brad himself tells the patrons he will be able to keep his store open.

Great stories – even about grisly topics – take viewers on a journey. They do not simply provide details; they engulf the audience in context and connection. Great storytellers understand this and frame their scripts with a narrative structure, building up to the grand moments their viewers will remember.

They also take the seemingly smaller steps to avoid tripping up their efforts.

Writing for TV

On the day I originally edited this chapter, the Los Angeles Times published an article that began with this sentence:

> The snitch who helped federal authorities decapitate Mexican Mafia operations within the Orange County Jail, and who is at the heart of allegations that the district attorney's office misused informants, was rewarded Friday for his cooperation with a break on potential prison time.
>
> (Goffard, 2016)

If you read the sentence in your head, it probably seems fine.

But try reading it out loud.

(Go ahead, try it ...)

It feels awkward, right?

It feels even more awkward to listen to it, mainly because it is so darn long. A print writer can get away with complex, layered sentences because a reader can more easily digest them. A TV writer cannot.

The first rule of writing for television is to write short, active sentences. I try to keep mine to 12 words or fewer. If I compose a longer sentence, I may break it up during editing with a NAT pop or quick sound bite.

(For reference, that Los Angeles Times sentence contains 43 words.)

I check myself on this with several tactics. When I reread my script, if I find a compound sentence, I break it in half. For example, if I have written a line like this:

> The robber left the bank ten minutes after he entered, stealing 100-thousand dollars and hundreds of gold bars.

I rewrite it as multiple sentences:

> The robber left the bank ten minutes after he entered. He stole 100-thousand dollars and hundreds of gold bars.

It is a simple trick that makes my script easier to read aloud.

When I write, I aim to never waste a word. My script above, for a story that lasted 100 seconds, features 295 words. This chapter, by comparison, features more than 6,000 words … and I still feel like I am leaving things out.

Most aspiring TV reporters learn a quick lesson when they start writing stories: they will never receive enough time to include every detail. But they can try, and they will have a better chance to at least partially succeed if they eliminate superfluous words.

One such word? "That."

When Land looks over a script, he looks for every instance of the word "that" and erases it. The absence of the word rarely alters the meaning of its sentence. For example:

> He said that he wanted to do something great.

Becomes:

> He said he wanted to do something great.

Or:

> Partridge looked to convince voters that she was the most qualified candidate.

Becomes:

> Partridge looked to convince voters she was the most qualified candidate.

The trick does not work every time; "that" is a word with many uses and meanings. When it does work, it saves valuable seconds.

It also provides a more granular example of an overall mindset. TV reporters must remain unsentimental as they determine what to include in a story. They must resist the urge to cram in as many pieces of information as possible, opting instead to highlight the most important points in a digestible way.

The final tip? End your sentences with power words. I have heard countless reporters and teachers convey this advice, and I regard it as one of the easiest and most effective tools for writing an engaging story.

Basically, the advice goes, when you write any sentence, you should figure out its most important and attention-grabbing part and end with it.

To illustrate this point, I present three sentences, all providing the same information:

- Johnson walked into his home to find a brown bear standing in his kitchen.
- Johnson found a brown bear standing in his kitchen when he walked into his home.
- Johnson walked into his home to find, standing in his kitchen, a brown bear.

Read each sentence aloud, and try to determine which one packs the biggest punch.

I imagine you will choose the third.

The most ear-catching part of this sentence is, clearly, the brown bear. That's the part you want to emphasize. Think of it as the punch line of your sentence.

(That last sentence, for example, would have sounded far better had I written, "Think of it as your sentence's punch line." "Punch line" is that sentence's ... punch line.)

Each of these steps usually involves taking time to reread your script. Under the deadline crunch, reporters often feel tempted to skip this part. They instead race to the audio booth, knock out their voice track, and allow as much time as possible for editing. But if you can spare a few minutes, you should. You will likely notice a handful of potential adjustments to either individual sentences or the overall structure.

Perhaps you can tell, from reading this chapter, my passion for writing. While I believe every step matters in the storytelling process, I particularly prize this one. My most memorable stories have hinged on great writing. When I think back, for example, to my NBC Nightly News piece about the man who saved a baby on the side of the road, I realize it succeeded because of how I wrote it. I shot some good video, and I edited a good package, but most importantly, I wrote a great script.

It's why people still remember that story years later. It's why I still think so fondly, nearly two decades later, about "Her Blue Haven."

And it's why I felt the need, nearly two decades earlier, to sit down at my Iowa bedroom computer and send its author a thank-you note.

Writing almost always wins the day.

References

Goffard, C. (2016, March 5). "With Prosecutors' Blessing, a Jailhouse Informant Tied to the Mexican Mafia Gets Leniency" [Newspaper Article]. Retrieved from www.latimes.com/local/orangecounty/la-me-oc-jailhouse-snitch-20160305-story.html

Land, T. (2015, January 10). "Volunteers Help Flood Victims in Aberdeen, Hoquiam" [Video File]. Retrieved from www.king5.com/story/news/local/2015/01/10/volunteers-help-flood-victims-in-aberdeen-hoquiam/21573665/

Pearl, M. (2013, December 19). "'Cabbagetown Christmas Miracle' Saves Little's Food Store" [Video File]. Retrieved from http://downtown.11alive.com/news/news/529562-cabbagetown-christmas-miracle-saves-littles-food-store

Pearl, M. (2015, April 13). "Falcons Stadium Price Tag Jumps Again, to $1.5 Billion" [Video File]. Retrieved from www.11alive.com/story/news/local/downtown/2015/04/13/falcons-stadium-price-billion/25736401/

Plaschke, B. (2002). "Her Blue Haven," in R. Reilly (ed.), *The Best American Sports Writing 2002*, pp. 1–10. Boston, MA: Houghton Mifflin.

Reilly, R. (2002). "Introduction," in R. Reilly (ed.), *The Best American Sports Writing 2002*, pp. xvi–xvii. Boston, MA: Houghton Mifflin.

Thompson, C. (2015, March 6). "That Way We're All Writing Now" [Web Log Post]. Retrieved from https://medium.com/message/that-way-we-re-all-talking-now-49e255037f15#.bamznitc3

Editing the Final Product

9

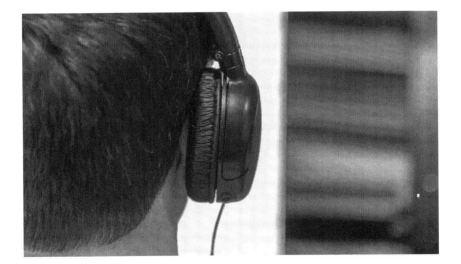

Figure 9.1

Credit: Nicole Leffer

Too often, I hear solo video journalists describe their days as individual marathons – with editing as the final mile.

I get the idea. Every step of the do-it-all process can be demanding: sometimes physically, sometimes emotionally, and always mentally. By the time one sits down to edit, one feels the time crunch and adrenaline push to complete a story. The deadline begins to feel like a finish line.

Such a description does a tremendous disservice.

During the last chapter, I said one's writing is perhaps the most important ingredient to telling a great story. It is, though, just an ingredient – like the sound bites, video clips, and other elements one spends the day gathering.

Editing is where one combines all of those ingredients to make the perfect dish.

Every decision as an editor can affect a viewer's perception. You can write the most poignant line of script but sabotage it by marrying it to the wrong shot of video. You can shoot an elaborate sequence but cut it in a way that doesn't make sense. You can capture a terrific piece of natural sound on camera but not make it loud enough for your viewer to hear.

An editor possesses immense power. Why should the editing process feel like an afterthought?

The best MMJs I know often enter the day with two deadlines: the deadline of when they must complete a story, and the earlier deadline of when they must begin to edit it. They leave plenty of time for editing because they understand its importance. When interns at my station shadow me for a day, they almost always seem surprised by the speed and seriousness with which I edit. I move swiftly and precisely, clacking away at the keyboard and darting my eyes around the screen. I become less talkative and far more focused. Sometimes I try to explain what I am doing, but I can never keep up with how quickly I am doing it.

Editing seems simple, and it can be simple. But it can also be a symphony.

It is where a day's work comes together. It is where a story develops its rhythm, flow, and true impact. Solo video journalists need to grasp the power in this part of the process, because our work will often succeed or fail because of it.

And you don't want to bust your butt all day to blow it on the final mile.

Forrest Sanders (Figure 9.2) views editing through a different lens:

"It's kind of like therapy."

Specifically, the award-winning soloist at WSMV-TV in Nashville will occasionally come to the station on his day off, sit down at his computer, and assemble a long-form package free of a looming deadline.

"Those are my babies, man," Sanders told me. "Usually the pieces I do on my own time are features. It's not because I'm necessarily a 'features guy,' but if I am not getting to do a particular style of story very often, I start to crave it. Most of the time, we have to address such heavy subjects. Sometimes I just need to do something to take off some steam."

More often than not, Sanders' therapy turns into tremendous output.

Figure 9.2 Forrest Sanders.

Credit: Forrest Sanders

He has won armfuls of Associated Press awards and Emmys. He was named the NPPA's Solo Video Journalist of the Year in 2018. And he was once honored as a finalist for the NPPA's Ernie Crisp Award for Photographer of the Year – a rare distinction for an MMJ.

Not bad for a guy who first noticed editing while watching a horror film.

"There was something about *The Evil Dead*," he recalls. "It had a shoestring budget but was shot in an interesting way that elevated the material. When I watched, it sort of flipped a switch in my brain. All of a sudden, shot composition and editing became a focus for me."

That focus still holds today, whether watching movies or creating his own work, which thrives on smooth rhythm and seamless editing.

Sanders and I have crossed paths several times through the years, but I first met him by interviewing him for this book. I learned we had independently developed many of the same philosophies and techniques for editing. I should not have been surprised – I could tell from his work the earnestness with which he edits – but I could not believe how often he said something that caused me to nod and say to myself, "Exactly!" This chapter will be longer than most, but it is full of terrific advice for making stories sing. It reflects the priority with which solo video journalists should view the editing process.

"The way you shoot, the way you edit, it does matter," said Sanders. "It can't just be something you throw together in ten minutes."

For that reason, one's first step to a great edit is deceptively simple: watch the clock.

Setting the Table

I have probably mentioned in every chapter the importance of time management. I have stressed how, throughout a given day, a solo video journalist must continually keep track of and project how much time he or she needs for each step.

Here is where that work pays off.

"It's more important to us than for a two-person crew," says Sanders. "Time management is everything, because if you lose track or don't pay attention to it, you could just ruin your story and get rushed at the very end."

A traditional photographer can relax a bit before editing, waiting for the reporter to log and write a script. An MMJ gets no such break, which often leads to that "final mile" feeling. That means setting a pre-editing deadline and sticking to it as best you can. How you choose that deadline all depends on how quickly and efficiently you edit. For example, if I get rushed or face any number of curveballs, I know I can cut a 90-second story in 20–30 minutes. Ideally, though, I like to give myself at least an hour, including whatever time I will need to send my story to the station's server for air. If I am working remotely, I consider the various complications that could occur – weak signal, slower feed process, etc. – and allow even more time.

My goal is to give myself room to not just edit the story but edit it well – a frequent challenge given our business's chaotic nature.

As Sanders says, "Much of the time, you feel a bit compromised, usually because time gets in the way."

You cannot fight time, but you can do your best to maximize it. You start by understanding your environment, from your physical location to your editing software.

Regarding the former, a one-person crew can work anywhere from a desk in the newsroom to the passenger seat of a car. Most coffee shops have great Wi-Fi connections, and I always feel more logistically comfortable with a chair and chai latte than by the side of the road. I typically prefer to edit in the newsroom, but I almost always bring my laptop on the road for shoots. That way, if I find myself pressed for time or facing a late return to the station, I retain the option to work in the field.

I also keep in mind my software – and how much I plan to push it.

Non-linear editors provide a seemingly infinite amount of effects, from color correction and visual transitions to image stabilization. With the software I use, these effects require minutes I do not always possess. I must then either allow more time for editing or approach my edit with fewer proverbial bells and whistles.

I try to leave time for one more step before I start: reminding myself what it's all about.

I can summarize my goals for any story into a four-point list:

1) I want people to watch my story.
2) I want people to understand my story.
3) I want people to be moved by my story.
4) I want people to remember my story.

I believe in, throughout the day, refocusing my mind and reestablishing why my story matters. I try to do so again before I edit, even when I find myself especially pressed for time. Many might not find this step necessary, but I find it essential in putting together a cohesive story – one where the whole is greater than the sum of my edits.

Sanders can sense when others' stories fail to meet those benchmarks.

"There are stories that stick with me," he says, "and there are stories that kind of play out in front of my eyes, where I don't take anything away from them."

As the editor, you craft your viewer's experience. You can never go wrong by reminding yourself why you want others to watch your work.

How you get them to watch – and understand, be moved by, and remember it – is more complicated.

Understanding the Basics

Editing is a difficult skill to both describe and define. Everyone seems to edit differently, from the software they use to the techniques they prefer. It also presents a somewhat steep learning curve, requiring a confidence and decisiveness often missing from inexperienced journalists.

"It just takes practice to get good at it," Sanders offers. "You're not going to be an editing whiz on day one, but if you are serious about it, you should work at it."

You should also work to master the step that, chronologically, occurs right before editing: recording the reporter's voice track.

I have underscored in several chapters the need to pay attention to not just video but audio. This obviously applies to the sound you obtain during your shoots, but it also relates to what you record in the audio booth (or, if working remotely, your car). Many reporters, MMJ or otherwise, rush through this step. I refuse to do so, and Sanders feels the same.

"I'm definitely not a one-take guy," he says. "I'll stand there and re-track a line over and over again until I feel like it's got the right emphasis or the right words. I don't want to sound bored. I listen to stuff I did a few years ago and think, 'I sounded halfway awake on that.'"

A great vocal track requires energy and empathy. While you, of course, want to remain objective with your emotion, you also want to sound like you care about your story and its subjects. Many find this difficult – not caring about their stories, but conveying that sincerity in the sterile, unnatural environment of an audio booth.

My advice? Use the 20% rule.

My first news director, Tedd O'Connell, was once a renowned anchor – the Ron Burgundy of Madison, Wis. – who possessed a gravelly, theatrical voice that resembled Al Pacino in *Scent of a Woman*. One day, as I prepared to head out for my first live shot for KMEG-TV, O'Connell called me into his office and said the following;

"Matt, when you go out there, you're gonna be really excited … so when you do your live shot, do it with about 20% less energy than you think you should."

He then added, in full Pacino, "Otherwise, you're gonna sound CRAAAAAAZY!"

That advice worked for me during my first live shots. For newcomers in the audio booth, I recommend the opposite.

When you do not feel the adrenaline of live television – and instead feel the insulation and isolation of the booth – you might be tempted to pull back your emotion. You might also feel awkward or uncomfortable with the idea of "selling" a story with your voice. In these situations, you should try to record your track with 20% more energy than you feel you need, experimenting until you reach the right level.

Otherwise, as O'Connell might have said, "You're gonna sound LAAAAAAZY!"

"It's about overcoming that boredom," says Sanders. "If I am sitting in a car or something, it's harder for me to get that energy than when I'm standing, even at a booth in the station. You want to be impartial to the story, so you do need to watch your inflections. At the same time, you want to sound like you are interested in what you are talking about."

You must also keep track of your audio's technical quality. When recording, either in the booth or into your camera, you should check your audio levels to make sure they do not get too high and cause distortion. Particularly when recording in the field, you should seek a location without much background noise where you can project loudly. Many MMJs, Sanders and myself included, do so in our cars.

Most importantly, I try to speak in a way that is digestible for the viewer. I emphasize certain words – most often, my sentence's power words – and never rush through my tracks. I treat my voice like an instrument to help guide my viewer, and I aim for clarity and confidence as I produce the final ingredient in my story's recipe.

Then I begin to cook.

I start with a step that often seems counterintuitive to newer editors: I lay down the tracked audio first.

Before we dive into this subject, let's establish some terminology. Most non-linear editors present you with a timeline for your project. The timeline typically includes a handful of tracks: several for video and several for audio. In a basic story, an editor will utilize three tracks:

- Video (V): An editor uses this space to lay down all the video clips in the story.
- Audio channel 1 (A1): An editor reserves this track for the story's voices, from its interview subjects to her or his reporter track.
- Audio channel 2 (A2): An editor fills this track with the story's other sounds, namely the NAT pops and background noise in his or her shots.

This matches how most photojournalists shoot a story: using audio channel 1 to record interviews, typically with a lavaliere microphone, and audio channel 2 to record natural sound, usually with a shotgun mic or the built-in mic on the camera.

Many younger journalists, when they start editing, attempt to edit the video and audio simultaneously. They will, for example, lay down a line of reporter track on A1 and then cover it with video – and the accompanying natural sound on A2 – before continuing to the next sentence or sound bite.

This takes way too long.

Nearly every editor I know simplifies the process. They lay down the tracked audio to A1 and then circle back, going through the timeline a second time to lay down the video and natural sound.

How does this help? Aside from being more efficient, it enables an editor to get a better sense of a story's rhythm – Does the script make sense? Does each line flow into the next? – and its length.

"I will go ahead and put down all of my audio track, then all of the SOTs," says Sanders. "Once I have all of it down on my timeline, that will give me a good indication: 'Do I need to trim this?'"

I often find I need to trim my stories. My script might seem on paper like that of a 90-second package but translates on a timeline to 1:45. I must then figure out what to remove – or call my producer with enough advance notice to ask for extra seconds.

Then I start the much longer process of laying down my video. I always aim to crush the introduction.

I wrote last chapter about the importance of "getting 'em in the tent," or writing an opening line or set of lines that command people's interest. You should provide similar attention to the video that surrounds these lines.

"I do think you need to grab people from the beginning," Sanders says. "Hopefully, then, they are along for the ride."

Studies have proven this true, on air and especially online. If a viewer is not captivated by a story's first few seconds, he or she will almost always turn it off. Thus, most editors use these seconds to unveil as many attention-grabbers as possible: a stirring NAT pop, a series of quick cuts and distinct sounds, or a captivating singular shot (think sunsets, landscapes, and other scene-setters, as in Figure 9.3).

Figure 9.3 Welcome to Broadway in downtown Nashville.

Credit: Karen Stoltz

They almost always refuse to begin a story with the reporter's first words. They will, instead, find some form of natural sound to both grab viewers' attention and place them in the environment of the story.

Sanders did this beautifully in a four-minute feature called "So Long, Mandolin Mike."

The titular character had worked as a street performer in downtown Nashville for nearly two decades, playing his signature stringed instrument, but now he was preparing to retire.

"His whole thing," Sanders recalls, "was, 'I am part of the culture of downtown.'"

How did Sanders reflect this? By not saying a word for 15 seconds.

He filled that time, instead, with this series of sights and sounds:

- 0:00: wide shot, with gentle ambient noise, of sunrise on Broadway in Nashville
- 0:02: quick tight shot, with more ambient noise, of a parking meter with blurred sunrise-tinted lights in the background
- 0:03: wide shot of the sunrise itself
- 0:04: tight shot, and accompanying sound, of a hand opening an instrument case
- 0:05: tight shot and NAT pop of a brush wiping the street, joined by the rising sound of mandolin music
- 0:07: wide shot of the street-wiping, with the mandolin music getting louder
- 0:08: tight shot and NAT pop of a street vendor's hand sorting a stack of potato chip bags
- 0:09: car wipe (a transition where a car blurs across the screen, its motion and zippy sound providing a seamless segue from one shot to the next)
- 0:09: medium shot of a party bus driving by and its patrons cheering
- 0:10: tight shot of a vendor giving a customer a hot dog and saying, "There you are, sir …"
- 0:11: wide shot, from behind, of a singer's face approaching a microphone
- 0:12: tight shot of a stringed instrument, with the whole section continuing to feature mandolin music in the background
- 0:12: medium shot as the earlier customer expounds, "That's a hot dog …"
- 0:13: tight shot of the mandolin player's shadow on the ground
- 0:14: one more tight shot of the player's hand picking the mandolin's strings.

Finally, at 0:15, Sanders' voice kicks in: "Downtown Nashville is alive" (Sanders, 2015).

He has spent the past 15 seconds proving it.

"I wanted the energy to kind of explode," he says in retrospect. "I wanted quick cuts, music coming from the honky-tonks – the energy that is downtown Nashville."

He showed that energy through the above sequence, which may seem elaborate but both commands interest and sets the mood.

If you can achieve those results, you might just convince your viewers to stick around for the rest.

Using Your Building Blocks

What do you do once you get them there?

Use the tools that got you here.

A compelling introduction might complete Goal 1 (getting people to watch your story), but it does not accomplish Goals 2–4 (getting people to understand it, be moved by it, and remember it). To do that, the best solo video journalists often rely on the fundamental techniques that have served them throughout the day.

One such technique? Editing with sequences.

When I watch one of my stories on the 6 PM news, I do so with the benefit of context. I have spent the whole day working on the story, and I can remember the location and background of every shot and sound bite. The viewer, in contrast, only experiences a story during the 90 seconds when it airs. If I hope to engage my audience, I need to write and edit my package in a way that enables people to immediately understand and care about what they are watching.

Sequences provide, in a short window, visual context.

"They do add something to the story," Sanders says. "When that effort is apparent, it really brings me into it. I start paying attention to what the story is about."

Look at the above introduction to Sanders' piece about Mandolin Mike. The 15 shots I listed comprise a series of sequences:

- The sunrise (three shots)
- The street-wiping (two shots)
- The exchange between a hot dog vendor and customer (three shots, counting the one where the vendor adjusts the bags of potato chips)

- The mandolin player opening his instrument and beginning to play (four shots, plus the continued drive of string music in the background).

The various sequences combine to immerse the viewer in the activity of downtown Nashville. Someone who has never stepped foot on Broadway can, after 15 seconds, visualize it in terms of sight, sound, and vibe. Sanders continues this throughout the story, attaching tight shots to wide shots and vice versa. He leads the viewer and refuses to use images that would seem out of context or difficult to place.

He also follows another basic but extremely important rule: match your video to your words.

"I don't know if I could imagine writing something at this point without knowing what the [accompanying] video will look like," Sanders says. "Your shooting informs your writing, and that informs the way you edit. After my script is done, I know all of the shots I'm going to edit to those segments."

I feel similarly with most of my stories, but I occasionally arrive at a sentence that does not lend itself to an obvious piece of complementary video.

In that case, I circle back to my log.

If I have done a thorough job with that step, I usually find a shot or NAT pop that will fit my script. Sanders surveys his logs – and cycles through his video while editing – for another reason: "I scour through the moments I want to make sure I put into the package, like the little bits of NAT sound that need to be in there."

Once you find them, you want to emphasize your most powerful moments in a meaningful way.

A few years back I was assigned to cover the homecoming of Emily Bowman, a 19-year-old who had been hit by a drunk driver four months earlier and, on this day, would finally return from the hospital. My producers pitched this as a heartwarming story. They described it with words like "great," "beautiful," and "uplifting."

The reality was far more complicated. Bowman had spent three weeks in a coma. Despite improvement and increasing stability, she could not walk and could barely move her muscles.

Her arrival – the presumed climax of my story – was one of the most complex, raw, and difficult moments I have ever witnessed.

Bowman's facial expression remained motionless. Her family and friends, amidst their hope and love, could not hide their sadness. They viewed her homecoming as the furthest thing from a happy ending. They saw, instead, one small step on the long, permanent road that awaited the rest of her life.

Every local station covered Bowman that day, but the other reporters all chose to run her arrival at the start of their stories. They essentially made the easy choice: lead with your best video, even if you have done nothing to set up for your viewer why that video is particularly special.

I did something different. I set up the moment by both describing its context and incorporating the mixed emotions of the people involved. I purposely avoided showing any video of present-day Bowman while discussing her past, instead using photographs to convey the personality and glow she displayed before getting hit by that driver.

Then I showed her arrival – a moment soaked in complexity and conflicted emotion. I let it run longer than any other shot. I wanted its power to truly sink in.

That's how to magnify your moments: setting them up with the proper background and then, as Sanders says, "stepping back and letting the moment tell itself."

When I edit a moment like Bowman's arrival, I rarely talk over it or lay someone's sound bite on top. I almost always show it raw. If that means the story might run a bit long, I alert my producer ahead of time. If I make a good enough argument – and possess a powerful enough moment – the producer will rarely say no.

"I suppose there are some places that have a hard-and-fast rule that [a package] can be only 1:30, maybe 1:15," Sanders offers. "But I think most of us are after the goal of creating good, compelling television."

Nothing gets more compelling than a beautifully presented moment.

Fine-Tuning the Product

The best editors, though, don't stop with sequences and moments.

They take whatever steps they can in whatever time they have to make their stories pristine and powerful.

Of course, sometimes even the best can go overboard, especially if they fail to focus on serving the story.

"When I was coming up, I wanted to prove [to my co-workers], 'I can do this,'" Sanders recalls. "I got into this thing of, 'Well, I'll show you that I can edit.' I really tried to overcompensate, meaning I was trying to throw every single editing trick I knew into my stories. Looking back, I'm like, 'Man, that story became kind of a circus.'"

Sanders learned what most eventually do: know about special effects, but use them with restraint.

"You have to ask yourself," he says, "'Is the way I'm cutting this going to supplement this story, or is it going to be a look-what-I-can-do distraction?'"

I went through a similar transition in my early years. For a long while, whenever I put together a longer feature, I supplemented it with music. I started each story with a jangly guitar or scene-setting piano and found a similar music bed to use at the end. Gradually I moved away from that philosophy, relying instead on natural sound and tighter editing to generate true emotion from my audience. I only use music today if it fits the tone of my story. For example, I recently put together a four-minute piece about the bombing of The Temple, a major synagogue in Atlanta and one of the city's most vibrant centers of Judaism. Most of my footage came from photos taken 60 years earlier, so I felt I needed to use music – to both provide some sort of background sound and propel forward an otherwise aurally poor story.

Most non-linear editing software includes a myriad of effects, from filters to transitions to plug-ins. You should become familiar with all of them, even if you will never use most. You will likely discover certain effects you can utilize frequently and efficiently that enhance, not distract from, your story's subjects.

"The shooting and the editing needs to be supporting [your subjects]," Sanders says, "and bringing you into their world. It cannot be you on the other end of the computer screen, flailing your arms around trying to get people's attention. That's not what storytelling is about. It's about letting them take center stage."

The effects I use most are the ones that prevent my stories from standing out negatively:

- Color correction: My camera shoots a relatively flat image, which means I must treat the color of my video until it adequately reflects how the scene looked in reality.
- Image stabilization: I am a stickler for this. If I find myself with a shot of shaky video, I use whatever effect I can to steady it out.
- Title tool: This allows me to write words on the screen, subtitle interviews spoken in other languages, and create my own graphics. (I use it often for social media posts.)
- Audio correction: I try to remove any hiss or feedback from my interview sound.

Speaking of sound, I focus as much on the audio as the video, specifically with transitions. I like my audio to sound clean and smooth; I aim to avoid clipped sound bites and jarring aural changes. I do this by adding "tails" to each of my audio tracks. If a typical timeline looks like this (see Figure 9.4):

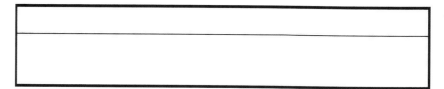

Figure 9.4 This audio cut will likely be harsh and abrupt.

Credit: Matt Pearl

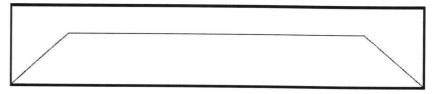

Figure 9.5 In this version, the audio will rise and fall gradually.

Credit: Matt Pearl

I extend the audio on either end of my clips and fade it in and out (see Figure 9.5).

By removing any harsh cuts, you enable the viewer to remain locked into your story. You get rid of any aural cues that would break someone's concentration. This is a subtle but essential technique – one on which Sanders places great importance.

"I don't like abrupt changes," he says. "I make sure there are audio transitions on all of it. I just try to make it seamless."

Finally, despite the hectic nature of the work and constantly looming deadlines, I constantly examine what works and what doesn't. I serve as my own toughest critic, rearranging video clips and removing sound bites and NAT pops that do not fit the story. I consider this a primary advantage of being a solo act. Because I control the whole process, I possess the autonomy to make whatever changes I like without requiring anyone's permission.

I will even, if I dislike the way I voiced a line of reporter track, run back to the audio booth and track it again.

"Sometimes I'll have something that sounds a little redundant, and I won't pick up on it until I'm in the edit," says Sanders. "If I feel like the energy needs to be boosted up, or perhaps it doesn't sound quite right for the somber quality of the story, I'll go in and re-track."

I almost always, during the course of my edit, make several decisions that would be much more difficult in a two-person crew. In the field, journalists in a two-person crew interact quite a bit. As the day continues, they rarely interact as frequently. A reporter typically writes the script with little input from the photographer, and the photographer typically edits without the reporter's presence. Solo video journalists operate in a different space. They can be self-contained units, controlling their stories during these influential steps. For example, a traditional photographer usually checks with the reporter before removing a line of script, but I can do that in a second. A traditional reporter will never know, until a story airs, whether her or his voice track sounds appropriate for the tone of the piece. I find out while I edit, in real time.

After I complete my story, I exercise my autonomy for one last process.

The Final Check

Let's go back to that analogy of a marathon.

If too many journalists treat editing as the final mile, perhaps just as many treat the moments after completing a story as the final 100 yards: they just put their heads down and sprint to the finish.

The best storytellers refuse to think that way.

Instead, after completing their packages but before delivering them for air, those storytellers rewatch their stories and hunt for potential issues.

Perhaps "check your work" falls into the same category of advice as "eat your vegetables": practical and important, yes, but entirely joyless, particularly when dessert – or a completed workday – is just minutes away.

That may seem true, but you do not want to feel the stomach ache of airing a story with a glaring mistake.

I actually aim, when possible, to rewatch my story twice. On the first round, I search for any obvious editing mistakes, such as:

- A flash frame: The blank frame that appears when two video clips do not border each other on the timeline.
- A jump cut: The continuity break that occurs when two shots from similar angles are edited back to back. It feels, to the viewer, like a "jump" in time.
- A/V sync errors: Sound bites where the video and audio do not match, resulting in a person's voice not matching the movement of his or her lips.

Mostly, though, I try to examine the overall flow of the piece. Does it feel right? Does it make sense? How can I improve it – usually in a tiny amount of time – before I send it to air?

"The timing of our job doesn't always lend itself to that," says Sanders, "but you try. I'll look at the video and make sure the timing of the shots looks right. Sometimes it will feel a little jarring to me, like maybe I edited one section too tightly. It's just polishing it up – trying to make it as good as I can."

Then, after that first run, I rewatch my story a second time, focusing specifically on audio.

"I'm kind of neurotic about the audio levels," Sanders says. "I have to make sure things are peaking just right – and that the natural sound isn't overwhelming my track."

I save this once-over for the end because I know I can skip it if need be. But I always benefit when I make time for it.

Then I send the final product to the server for air – ideally, with time to spare.

"I like to get it done about 15 minutes ahead of time," Sanders says. "Technical snafus are bound to happen. We're working with technology."

This is very true, especially when working remotely. But a 15-minute cushion also gives you time to prepare for, if you have one, your live shot. You can go to the bathroom, apply and check your make-up, put on a suit jacket or blazer, and reread your script. You might even be able to take a few deep breaths and relax before you go on live television.

Then, after your story airs, you can savor your accomplishment.

I feel a certain satisfaction every time I watch a finished package. Even if only for a second, I acknowledge that I have just created something from scratch and put it on television. In most cases, I have done so by myself, which makes the victory especially sweet.

"I can't really imagine doing one of them without the other," says Sanders of the traditional news roles. "I don't know how many people are multimedia journalists and actually love this, but I feel like we are kind of a rare breed."

I love many aspects of the solo life, but I especially love that seemingly daily feeling of fulfillment. Sometimes, at the end of the day, I do feel like I have completed a marathon – one I will recreate 24 hours later. But I always appreciate the process and the product.

I encourage you to do the same.

Reference

Sanders, F. (2015, September 30). "So Long, Mandolin Mike" [Video File]. Retrieved from www.youtube.com/watch?v=KtCjIiW6YiO

Career Chronicles

Getting in at an Older Age

In 2008 Peter Rosen received the National Press Photographers Association's Best of Photojournalism Award for Reporting.

That same year, he lost his job.

"They laid off a bunch of us," Rosen recalls. "It was a difficult time for a lot of people."

Rosen had worked at KUTV in Salt Lake City for nearly two decades, developing a tremendous reputation as a feature reporter with a knack for creative, unorthodox storytelling. But when the national economy went south, during already lean times for local TV news departments, Rosen became a casualty. He remained unemployed two years later, scratching together a set of freelance gigs as a commercial producer and editor but unable to find a full-time job as a traditional reporter.

Frustrated and weary, Rosen posted on his personal blog a "Where is he now?" entry that ended with:

> Feature reporting isn't what it used to be.
> Courage.

(Rosen, 2010)

When Rosen finally received another shot – two years later at fellow Salt Lake station KSL-TV – he decided to take a more modern approach.

"I was basically hired as a video producer/reporter," he recalls, "but I said to the news director at the time that I'd like to be able to shoot some of my own stuff. I thought it was a good job skill, and I thought it would give me job security or some other skills I could use if I were ever to be laid off again."

How did the news director respond? "With an emphatic, 'Yes! We would love for you to do that.'"

That's how Rosen became a solo video journalist ... at age 51.

In some ways, I was lucky.

I entered the journalism business with few expectations of becoming a traditional reporter – at least not right away. I heard numerous times in college that I should prepare to – during my first and second jobs – shoot and edit my own stories. Beyond that, I originally wanted to work as a sports anchor and reporter, and I knew that most local sports departments featured small staffs that necessitated one-person crews. I had not arrived at school with the intention of learning how to shoot video. By the time I left, I knew I would need to master it.

But at least, I felt, I would not need to unlearn how to do otherwise. I would be able to acquire the necessary skills – and live through whatever mistakes I would make in the process – in my 20s in a small market, not in my 40s and 50s in a large market.

Basically, I had not yet gotten comfortable in my career, so I saw no issue with getting uncomfortable.

But many experienced reporters and photographers, who entered the business decades earlier at a time of little change in TV news, now find themselves flooded with new expectations. A generation raised without social media has been forced to learn Facebook, Twitter, and Instagram. Reporters who for years produced one story for TV must now write web stories, upload photos and video from their cell phones, and post constant updates online throughout the day.

A rising number of older journalists are taking on one more challenge: unlearning the cushier role of a traditional reporter or photographer and adopting the solo mantle.

Back in Chapter 1, I mentioned one of my co-workers, Jon Shirek, who was asked by his news director to become an MMJ after nearly three decades as a top-shelf reporter. Shirek told me he accepted the role with hesitation.

"I didn't want to have to do something new," said the multi-award-winning journalist. "I didn't think I could be good at it. I was working with great photographers who knew how to tell a story and loved to tell a story visually, and that was wonderful. Everything was going well. I didn't want to shake things up."

Before Rosen lost his job, he too balked at the idea.

"When MMJs started really popping up" in the early to mid-2000s, said Rosen. "I was worried about it, not for myself but for the implications for the business. It works in some instances but doesn't work in all instances. I think there was fear, and I probably was among those people, because I thought, 'Every news director is going to want to do this.'"

For himself, though, Rosen (Figure CC3.1) did not mind the idea. He had always enjoyed editing his own stories, and on the rare occasion where he had picked up a camera, he had excelled. In 2007 Rosen wanted to do a story about a woman who took photographs with archaic plastic cameras. When no KUTV photographers were available to shoot it, Rosen picked up a point-and-shoot camera and shot it himself.

As he says, "I MacGyvered it."

The story wound up winning an award for photography.

Rosen recalls the pleasantly surprised reactions of his co-workers: "Someone in the control room said to me, 'Wow, those colors look great. What kind of camera are you using?' I purposely didn't advertise it because I didn't want us to switch to only $100 cameras."

Five years later, when Rosen decided to weave shooting and editing into his day-to-day life, he found an environment much more friendly to one-person

Figure CC3.1 Peter Rosen.

Credit: Peter Rosen

crews. In the 1980s, he says, "we were using heavy wooden tripods and had bags for lights, and it just didn't look feasible at that point in time."

Now, even though Rosen is in his late 50s with self-described lower-back issues, he says "the camera is light enough that it doesn't cause problems."

Physically he has not felt burdened. Mentally he has felt invigorated.

"For me, personally, it's a mind–body experience," Rosen says before launching into one of the most existential descriptions I have ever heard of life as a solo video journalist. "Before I shoot, I'm kind of nervous, because I am afraid I'm going to mess up because I don't have as much confidence in my skills. But once I'm into it, I'm so absorbed in what I'm doing that I forget what time it is, and time just flies by. My brain's working, and my body's working. It employs everything I have … and maybe something I don't have."

That "something" is the feeling of mastery over his craft – or, perhaps more precisely, the sense of comfort and predictability that seems to develop more easily in traditional reporters.

"It takes a lot of concentration and a lot of physical skill to be able to shoot it right," Rosen says. "You're thinking about the camera and the technical aspects of shooting. At the same time, you're trying to think of how you're going to write the story. At the same time, you're trying to be a person and converse with somebody. At the same time, you're trying to be a reporter and get the information. At the same time, you're trying to anticipate what's going on and what you're going to need to shoot. It just keeps your brain always thinking."

All of that work, Rosen says, leads to a fulfilling conclusion.

"The payoff comes when you're editing," he says. "It's a satisfying feeling to know you've got yourself a story."

Perhaps Rosen's description of the solo life, with its chaotic nature and constant juggling, sounds like an appetizing challenge.

If, however, you have grown accustomed to a more stable and established existence as a traditional reporter, such a description probably seems far removed from what you desire.

"I don't think most 54-year-old reporters are going out and trying to be MMJs," says Rosen. "It's not something you do when you haven't done it for your whole career."

And despite Rosen's success as a one-man band – he regularly wins NPPA awards for his memorable features – he does not view the concept as an all-encompassing solution. "I wouldn't want to cover spot news on a daily basis as an MMJ," he says.

But for an older reporter or photographer with any number of desires, from additional job security to a feeling of rejuvenation, going solo can be a worthy pursuit.

To those who take the plunge, Rosen offers this advice: "The best training for anybody learning to shoot is to first learn to edit. You learn how pictures go together, and you start thinking about how a photographer got that shot, what they had to do to get that shot, and how they sequenced a story. You watch their raw tape, so you see what they shot when. You learn what you like and don't like, and you develop your style."

Similarly, traditional photographers should approach writing with the knowledge that they already do it in a visual sense. They should dissect the scripts of the reporters whose stories they edit, then determine their own preferences and cultivate their own styles.

"Just about anyone can do it," Rosen says, "if they want to."

Those willing to handle some initial discomfort can discover far greater rewards. Feature reporting, as Rosen once wrote, is perhaps not what it used to be. In his case, it has become a new and uniquely rewarding chapter.

"Everyone wants to grow in their field, and this is a different way for me to grow."

Reference

Rosen, P. (2010, March 17). You Mean People Actually Read This? [Web Log Post]. Retrieved from www.featurereporter.com/2010/03/you-mean-people-actually-read-this.html

Part IV

Looking Forward

The MMJ Survey

10

Figure 10.1

Credit: Matt Pearl

The year after publishing the first edition of *The Solo Video Journalist*, I crafted a multi-page questionnaire to better understand how soloists view their jobs. I dubbed it the MMJ Survey, and I heard from nearly a hundred soloists nationwide with diversity in age, gender, and market size. They offered responses that often showed a clear consensus – and unearthed some conclusions I found surprising and often unsettling. I had debated whether to include it here, in a book that's far more about the fundamentals and practical tools of solo storytelling.

Then I heard about Paige Pauroso.

In November 2019, the MMJ was five months into her second job when she was assaulted in the field. Pauroso had stopped along a busy block to shoot B-roll – "I just needed video of a street," she told me – when a woman approached with foul language and demanded she stop recording. Pauroso tried to talk her down, and the woman eventually walked away. But as Pauroso collected her final shot, the woman returned, followed her, and smacked her in the back of the head with an open hand. The force pushed Pauroso's head into her camera and left her with a bruise. The woman turned around and left. Pauroso got in her car and did the same.

A day later Pauroso made her experience public. She posted on Twitter and Facebook. Journalists nationwide responded. Most expressed sympathy and support, but many used her story to decry the use of MMJs altogether. Pauroso, for her part, gave context to her solo status when she posted about the incident. But when I interviewed her a month later, she offered a perspective that made me realize why my MMJ Survey remains critical reading for incoming one-person crews.

"I used to joke at my old station that I didn't sense fear," Pauroso told me. "Before this incident happened, I did not feel very fearful out in the field. After it, I definitely learned you can't go into situations blindly. You can't assume every situation is going to work out."

Pauroso (Figure 10.2) said her managers had always told her she could bail on a story if it didn't seem safe. But she never followed through. That changed after her assault. She told me of two instances in the previous week where her story would have sent her to areas known for crime and drug deals – except this time, she called it off.

"It hasn't made me more fearful," she told me. "It has made me more aware. I'm not scared to do my job, but I am a little more on guard, which is a good thing."

Pauroso's encounter – and the industry-wide response – underscores the need for MMJs to empower themselves and find community amongst each other. Outsiders often belittle the position and view it as a two-for-one combo package of reporter and photographer. But solo video journalists face unique challenges not experienced by – and not immediately obvious to – their colleagues in more traditional roles.

Figure 10.2 Paige Pauroso.

Courtesy of Paige Pauroso

The MMJ Survey offers a snapshot of how we fit into the local news landscape. It should also provide greater context for how the majority of our solo colleagues view their jobs. I'm not going to post the survey's entire results, but I will offer seven takeaways from its most salient responses:

1. The Highest Concentration of Responding MMJs Came from Top 25 Markets

One of the most outdated critiques of the MMJ concept – from those in traditional roles and MMJs themselves – is that it only exists in small and medium-sized markets. Many solo video journalists view the position as a means to an end. They think they must take the job when they start in the business but can leave it behind once they get to a big city.

The demographics of this survey show why that idea is largely false.

Nearly a quarter of the 96 MMJ Survey respondents worked in Top 25 markets. Nearly half worked in Top 50 markets. How does that affect them? Here were some of the responses:

- "I have resources on which I can lean if needed."
- "[It's] very fast-paced, and a lot is expected out of one person at times."
- "Traffic and driving eats up considerable amounts of time … It was easier to MMJ in smaller to medium markets in my opinion, but the work you put in there sets you up for the larger markets."

- "I work in a market where most people don't MMJ, so my product is compared to one done by three people."
- "I have insanely good MMJs to compete against. You really have to step up your game."

Overall, the solo concept has undeniably found a home in big markets. As one solo video journalist wrote, "MMJs are becoming standard. Other stations used to make fun of my station for MMJing, but now all of them do it."

2. MMJs, By and Large, Feel Confident about Their Abilities to Do Their Jobs and Manage Their Time

I asked respondents to rate, on a scale of 1 to 7, whether they agreed with a variety of statements about life as a solo video journalist.

I found MMJs don't lack self-confidence. The majority agreed with the following statements:

- "I have enough time during the day to fulfill the requirements of my job."
- "I feel confident in my ability to manage my time as an MMJ." (More than two-thirds of respondents gave that statement a 6 or 7, indicating particularly strong agreement.)
- "I regularly produce work that is better than that of traditional two-person crews in my market."

3. Most MMJs Enjoy Being MMJs

Respondents also largely gave high marks to the role itself. Nearly two-thirds agreed with the statement, "I enjoy being an MMJ," with nearly one-third giving that statement a full 7 out of 7.

Similarly, many soloists claimed they had received unique opportunities because of their solo status. At least three-quarters said they enjoy shooting B-roll, shooting and conducting interviews, and editing stories. Not a single respondent claimed to dislike writing.

This paints a relatively glorious picture of life as a solo video journalist.

It also makes the conclusion in the next heading extremely concerning.

4. The Majority of MMJs Don't See Themselves in This Role Ten Years from Now

I admit being surprised by this result, mainly because many of the others had been so positive. But when I asked people to rate the statement, "I see myself as an MMJ ten years from now," more than a third of respondents gave it a 1 out of 7: complete disagreement.

Of all the statements I presented, this one received the lowest rating by far. But it is supported by some of the survey's other responses:

- The vast majority of MMJs agreed with the statement, "I often feel overwhelmed with my workload."
- A noticeable majority disagreed with the statement, "My news director and managers understand the intricacies of being an MMJ."
- A similar majority (roughly two-thirds of respondents) also disagreed with the statement, "My industry values MMJs equally to traditional reporters and photographers."

This should give us pause. It essentially says local TV news possesses a workforce of eager, ambitious, talented solo video journalists who enjoy the job ... but don't see it as a long-term way of life.

Why? A few reasons follow.

5. Many MMJs, Particularly Women, Possess Significant Concerns about Safety

The statement, "I feel safe as an MMJ when in the field," received a lukewarm response.

News managers should, right away, consider this a cause for alarm. More than 40% of responding MMJs disagreed in some way about feeling safe. I view that as nowhere near an acceptable number, even if I do not necessarily place myself in that group.

(I also feel, in my newsroom, comfortable with speaking up when I sense an unsafe situation. Based on some of the comments from respondents in this survey, many soloists do not possess similar confidence.)

The numbers showed a noticeable divide in terms of gender. Male MMJs gave the statement about safety an average of 4.5, or slight agreement. Female MMJs gave it an average of 3.1, a much lesser vote of confidence.

It begs a seemingly obvious question: if an MMJ believes him or herself to be regularly unsafe on the job, why would he or she want to do that job?

6. Women Care for the MMJ Life Far Less than Men

The gender disparity in MMJ responses was not just limited to safety.

With nearly every statement, women gave a less favorable rating than men. What statements drew large gaps?

- "I have enough time during the day to be able to thrive at my job." On a scale of 1–7, male respondents gave that an average of 4.6; female respondents averaged 3.6.
- "My news director and managers understand the intricacies of being an MMJ." Male respondents averaged 4.2; female respondents averaged 3.0.
- "I have received unique opportunities because I am an MMJ." Men gave it an average of 5.0; women averaged 4.1.

But the largest disparity came with the statement referenced earlier: "I see myself as an MMJ ten years from now." Male respondents averaged 4.5; female respondents averaged 2.7.

This presents a major issue for our industry – an issue compounded by the fact that women make up the majority of MMJs. (At least, they did in this survey by 58% to 42%.) The journalism world will lose a great deal of talent if it does not address this.

7. MMJs Love Most Parts of the Job … but They *Hate* Solo Live Shots

The latest trend in solo video journalism is easily the most discouraging.

When I asked solo video journalists to rate their enjoyment and ability to perform the various tasks of the job, they gave nearly every task a positive overall response. The lone exception? Shooting their own live shots.

Look at these averages on a 1–5 scale:

How much do you enjoy the following tasks? (1 = do not enjoy; 5 = enjoy).

- Writing the story: 4.5
- Editing the story: 4.3

- Shooting B-roll: 4.1
- Shooting and conducting interviews: 4.1
- Being live on TV: 4.1
- Researching the story: 3.8
- Posting and engaging on social media: 3.6
- Shooting one's own live shot: 1.9.

How easy are the following tasks? (1 = most difficult, 5 = easiest)

- Writing the story: 3.9
- Shooting B-roll: 3.9
- Editing the story: 3.8
- Being live on TV: 3.8
- Shooting and conducting interviews: 3.7
- Posting and engaging on social media: 3.4
- Researching the story: 3.3
- Shooting one's own live shot: 2.1.

Again, this should be alarming.

Why the distaste for solo live shots? The lack of safety looms large. Many MMJs left comments like these:

- "People approach me and I feel unsafe. I like just having someone there."
- "I don't feel safe in many places, and there is no way to defend myself. I often go to a generic safe space and lose creativity so I know people will leave me alone."
- "I've had people curse at me and insult me because the producer in my ear has me on standby and Joe Viewer doesn't understand why I'm not talking back to him."
- "[It's] unsafe and often at scenes of murders."
- "MMJs are distracted from their surroundings for a little while … which isn't a great thing when live TV is such an attractor of crazy."

Beyond that, this seems to be the one area where solo video journalists do not feel they can replicate the quality of traditional crews. They find it limiting, static, and way too time-consuming, especially while on deadline.

In the end, solo live shots are symptomatic of a larger problem: many MMJs feel at best misunderstood, and at worst penalized, for their solo status.

The Open-Ended Truth

The MMJ Survey ended with a series of open-ended questions that I have included below. While I cannot publish every answer, I present below those that represent the most frequently heard themes from today's solo video journalists:

Question: List (up to) three things you LOVE about being an MMJ.

- "I like feeling accomplished when my story comes out great and it's all me."
- "[I love] owning the story from start to finish, being more agile, [and] being a step ahead of 2-man teams who need to conference to get on the same page."
- "I LOVE shooting. I LOVE writing. I LOVE editing. I love doing it all, and I know what I want my end product to look like, so I execute my vision."
- "I love the freedom it gives me to take risks, the ability to truly tell a story in my voice, and the satisfaction I get when I produce a great story and know I did it all by myself."
- "It whipped my time management skills into shape. I can envision something creative and run with it. It pushes me to get creative with shots and interviews."
- "I love being proud of my work from start to finish – that was ME who pulled off that story or got that great shot or made something creative out of a story that could have easily been cookie-cutter."
- "I truly love all parts of the process: research, shooting, social media, interviewing, writing, editing, presenting live, etc. and I'd be a little sad to lose some of them. I'd love working with a partner, but I'd miss shooting and editing."
- "[I love] not having to coordinate shoots around another person's schedule. Low-key production leads to more intimate connection with subjects."

My take: Nearly every response to this question featured some form of the words "freedom," "control," and "ownership." MMJs take advantage of the chance to set their own schedules and oversee a story from start to finish. They take pride in their abilities at the various tasks and their willingness to rise to the solo challenge.

QUESTION: List (up to) three things you CAN'T STAND about being an MMJ.

- "I don't feel safe a lot of the time and management does not care."
- "There are places where in-house staff wants me to go live that are not safe for me. I really feel alone in the car most days, especially on long distance assignments and severe weather coverage."
- "1. Carrying 50+ pounds of equipment. 2. The overwhelming workload 3. Not being able to focus as much on my writing."
- "I just wish there was more time in the day."
- "I can't stand the managers and producers who don't understand the challenges MMJs face, the constant remarks from reporters and photographers at other stations who pity me or look down at me for being an MMJ, and the fact that MMJs get paid significantly less than reporters even though we do the work of two people."
- "Solo live shots."
- "There's nothing I 'can't stand,' but there are days that time management is difficult. I set a very tight schedule for myself, and if one of my interviews shows up late, it does have more potential to derail my day than it would for a two-person crew."
- "[I can't stand] the physical demands, ruined clothing and awkward questions ('Where's your photographer!?' 'They make you carry that all by yourself??!') that reporters do not have to deal with."
- "1. The absolute ignorance from my producers and assignment workers as to what goes into my day and how much work I'm constantly doing. 2. The absolute ignorance of more veteran reporters and photogs who look down on me as a junior reporter trying to get to the next step when in reality this is exactly what I want to be doing. 3. The seeming inability or unwillingness of some managers and news directors to give MMJs a shot at being bigger players in the newsroom."
- "BURNOUT. Giving your all for a story in one day can take a lot. It's rewarding, but at the same time it can be difficult sustaining that same excellence day after day after day."
- "It looks unprofessional just to have one person doing everything. I feel like I never get to really dig deep into my stories because I am literally doing the work of 3–4 people."

My take: Plenty of MMJs cited concerns that might be expected: an overwhelming workload, too many responsibilities, and the physical toll of carrying gear. Many specifically mentioned their hatred for solo live shots.

Beyond that, I heard consistent themes of burnout and disrespect. Too many solo video journalists feel they are treated as lower-grade reporters, not multi-skilled reporters with unique strengths and challenges. They feel abused because of their versatility, not rewarded for it.

QUESTION: If I could impart one piece of knowledge to my non-MMJ coworkers about my job as an MMJ, it would be …

- "I wish they knew how dangerous this was. Doing door knocks or doing live shots when you're alone at murder scenes is not okay."
- "You all need to realize that there are some things I literally cannot do as one human being. I'm not trying to be lazy or bad at my job, but I cannot be in court and waiting outside with a camera at the same time, I cannot write my entire script and email it while driving, I cannot turn three stories that are all an hour apart from each other, and honestly I cannot answer your phone call every minute of the day."
- "Listen to your MMJs when they tell you it's too much. Most of us won't ask for a photographer unless we truly need one."
- "There are pros and cons to assigning certain stories to me, but it's important to know that the visual ones are often where you'll get your biggest bang for your buck."
- "When we say we don't feel safe or something unrealistic isn't likely to happen, don't think it's us being lazy or trying to get out of something. Trust us; we are doing it daily."
- "I prefer MMJing. I'm not a reporter still condemned to paying dues … who'd scramble at the chance to get out. It gives me purpose. I might ultimately be a cost-saving measure, but I'm cool with that."
- "I am literally doing the job of multiple people. Keep that in mind when you ask if I can please shoot you a tease or an extra something. I barely have time to breathe during the day. Odds are I do not have time to shoot anything extra for you, but I will say yes because I'm a team player and want to please."
- "I'M BY MYSELF, A******!"

My take: The comments feature a lot of specific advice, but they all revolve around a basic desire for understanding and respect. (The last response may be a more cathartic version of that request.) In my experience, solo video journalists are mostly willing to take on the extra workload … as long as it is deployed with a little common sense. I would encourage non-MMJs in the newsroom to talk with MMJs and try to develop an appreciation for the intricacies of the job. I would encourage the reverse as well. Solo video journalists should make their voices heard, but they should also express a willingness to learn how other positions operate.

QUESTION: If I could impart one piece of knowledge to my news director and managers about my job as an MMJ, it would be ...

- "I am sent to many situations where I do not feel safe, and it should be the manager's responsibility to acknowledge safety concerns."
- "Pay me more. I do the work of two people. I'm not asking to be paid double, but at least want to make as much as a standard male photographer (which I don't)."
- "I should be rewarded for making this job what you all want it to be – someone who is fiercely independent, producing memorable, unique, stories."
- "Talk with the MMJs on your staff. Set realistic expectations for the job. Offer MMJs on your staff feedback often. Working solo, they're the ones that want feedback the most – but don't always get it."
- "It's a real art. But people won't pursue it forever if it doesn't pay. And if you're stuck with talent who is only as good as bottom-level pay, people will stop watching."
- "Pulling off a three-package day is a miracle, even when I do it. It shouldn't be the expectation."
- "Young MMJs will break their backs trying to impress management. Praise goes a long way."
- "Give MMJs more opportunities to learn. Let us spend more time with the talented photojournalists you rely on. It's great to have everyone turn a package every day, but it can be more helpful in the long run to let us watch veterans work. Critiques only cover so much."
- "I care about the quality of my work so deeply. I am disappointed that it suffers sometimes because I don't have any help. Being an MMJ is not below being a reporter or an anchor. We are the hardest working and carry the most stress and pressure in the newsroom. We deserve just as much respect as our teammates."

My take: News directors and managers face the most responsibility to ensure a happy workforce and memorable product. With MMJs, they need to a set a tone that values safety and encourages their soloists to speak up when uncomfortable. They should also be on the lookout for ways to develop and educate. Several respondents said they would learn much more if given the occasional chance to work with a photographer (or a fellow MMJ).

Perhaps some of these responses and conclusions seem obvious. But too many paint a picture of doing twice the work for half the pay and credit.

This leads many solo video journalists to feel jaded and exhausted.

I have been fortunate to experience an early career filled with great successes and opportunities. I have traveled around the world and produced stories in which I take tremendous pride. But I credit my success, in large part, to news directors and managers that have seen the value in one-person crews and rewarded me for my versatility. Without such confidence and incentive from above, I doubt even I would have wanted to remain a solo act.

I encourage all of us to seriously rethink how we approach the MMJ position. Quite a few solo video journalists have carved out beautiful careers, but the majority – especially younger ones – feel overwhelmed, despite their passion for the job.

We cannot abuse such a vital part of our workforce. On the contrary, we must train and cultivate MMJs to enable them to shine in ways they clearly can.

Our profession is too important to do otherwise.

Learning from the Best **11**

Figure 11.1 Boyd Huppert.
Credit: Ben Garvin

A few chapters ago, San Diego multimedia journalist Joe Little made a point worth re-examining.

"I don't look up to MMJs," said one of the best in the industry. "I look up to photographers and reporters. I want people to think, 'This guy's got a crew of 15 people with him.' I don't want anybody giving me sympathy because I'm an MMJ."

You have likely heard a variation of that theme from many of the distinguished solo video journalists in this book.

Unfortunately, many one-person crews feel limited in what they can accomplish. They see the daunting demands in their job descriptions, but they also receive too much external discouragement that turns into internal doubt. Some colleagues immediately discount MMJs because of their status. Others denigrate the concept as the bane of the business.

Heck, even the people we interview often pity the fact that we do it all.

The best solo video journalists ignore such talk – and aim to rise far above it. They know their viewers draw no distinction between their work and that of traditional crews, so they too refuse to do so. They aim to put out the best stories, period, and they bristle at the idea of settling for less.

In that spirit, I present to you the person who has set the standard for storytellers everywhere: Boyd Huppert.

The longtime reporter for KARE-TV has become a fixture in the Twin Cities with his feature segment, "Land of 10,000 Stories." He has won more than 100 regional Emmys and 16 National Edward R. Murrow Awards. His work has appeared on CNN and NBC News.

He is not a solo video journalist.

Huppert has spent his career working with some of the finest photographers in the business. He has rarely, if ever, picked up a camera, and he regularly receives multiple days to craft the stories that win the aforementioned awards. When Huppert speaks at journalism conferences – and he has done so around the world – he never tailors his presentation for MMJs. He simply speaks about a far more universal concept.

"I'm teaching the elements of storytelling," Huppert says, "and those elements are as useful to a two-person or three-person crew as they are to an MMJ. The challenges are different for MMJs, but the stories aren't. I don't think what we're trying to achieve should be any different."

That outlook is exactly why I chose to interview him.

Throughout this book, I have examined how to negotiate the challenges and leverage the advantages of doing it all to produce compelling and powerful work. I fully acknowledge that life as a solo video journalist can be quite different from life in a two-person crew.

This chapter is a reminder to look past those differences. It is a reminder that the quality of what you produce has little to do with being a reporter or a photographer. It has a lot to do with being a journalist and a storyteller.

I reached out to Huppert in that spirit. He is, in so many ways, an exception to the norm of TV news, and he is a touchstone for any aspiring journalist looking to aim as high as possible. Over our conversation, he offered advice about the storytelling process that can benefit us all.

Treat Every Day as a Chance to Learn

Huppert is fond of saying he was not born with a journalism pedigree. ("I really have no business doing this," he told me. "I grew up on a dairy farm in Wisconsin.") He started in the profession like most of us: majoring in journalism, getting a job in a tiny market, and working his way up.

He got to where he is by using every opportunity to improve.

"It's been gradual," Huppert says. "I feel like I have just hit my stride in the last two years. I'm more consistent now. I feel like I'm getting it right on a more regular basis."

The secret to his success? "I think a lot of it is just reps – it's doing the same thing over and over and over and over."

But plenty of people work in the business for decades and produce numerous stories. Far fewer push themselves with each one. Huppert believes in the concept of continual education, which often occurs through the work he produces.

"I'll rewrite an ending four times before I'm happy with it," he said. "I'll show it to other people and ask if there's a better way I can write this. I'm very critical. I think that's a gift, because if you're not critical of your work, you're going to get stuck."

This holds particularly true for solo video journalists, who often feel so overwhelmed by their responsibilities that they focus on simply finishing their work rather than perfecting it.

"I don't think it's a good instinct to say, 'I'm as good as I need to be,'" says Huppert. "It's a better instinct to say, 'This could be better.'"

Don't File a Report; Tell a Story

How can you immediately make an assignment better? Adjust the way you approach it.

"A report is a collection of facts," Huppert says. "A report is an assignment. It's wire copy. It's a press release. I'm trying to find something with a soul.

That's a story. A story has characters and a plot line, and it has surprises. It's engaging in a way a report never could be."

So many aspiring journalists never receive that lesson. Huppert himself did not truly hear it until he looked outside of the newsroom.

"One of the best things I ever did," he recalls, "was attend the NPPA News Video Workshop in Norman, Oklahoma. I was convinced to attend, and that's where my eyes were really opened to the possibilities. I just came back and was like, 'I didn't know I could do that! I didn't know I could be a journalist and tell stories!' It really refocused my career."

As a one-person crew, again, you might feel compelled to skip this step in the storytelling process. You might be tempted to sprint out the door with a press release and focus only on completing your assignment. But if you don't train yourself to find the story in your report – the human connections, the subtle nuances, the societal implications – you will miss out on the chance to imbue your work with true meaning.

You also run the risk of assuming you know the story before you tell it.

"I worked with someone who wrote his stories before he went and shot them, because it was easier that way," Huppert said with a chuckle and, I imagine, a shake of the head. "I don't recommend that."

Plan Ahead, the Right Way …

I have discussed the importance of planning one's day from the standpoint of time management. It also enables one to brainstorm how to gather the ingredients of a great story.

"I think about the order in which we're going to shoot things," Huppert says, and then he will schedule his shoots as he sees best.

He offers, as an example, a beautiful story he produced one Valentine's Day:

> "I did this story about these two sisters that were cleaning out their parents' attic. As they were cleaning, they found these candy boxes from 68 years of marriage. Their dad gave their mom a heart-shaped box of candy every year.
>
> "What I have to determine is, 'How are we going to order this?' I think of it almost like acts in a play. Act One: we need to meet the daughters, but we don't want to meet the parents yet. So how could we see the

parents? Maybe through photo albums! Then we're going to go to the attic and see the [heart-shaped] boxes: that's Act Two.

"Act Three: now we're going to interview the parents. But I don't want the daughters there when we interview the parents. So I ask the daughters, 'Do you mind if we spend an hour with your parents?'

"Act Four: the daughters come over and see the parents."

When he thought of this schedule, Huppert had not yet met the daughters, and his photographer had not yet shot a frame of video. But they entered those shoots with a framework.

"Now the story doesn't just stand in place," Huppert said. "Now we're taking a little journey through a two-minute story. Those are the things I can plan."

But Allow Yourself the Chance to Be Surprised

Within that journey, Huppert refuses the urge to fill in the blanks himself.

"Almost everything good in every story I've ever done has surprised me, and then it's my job to allow the viewers to feel that same surprise," he says. "I don't want to plan to the point that I can't be surprised."

In Huppert's best stories – heck, in most reporters' best stories – the people within them receive the room to fully express themselves. If you arrive with a preconceived notion of what you hope someone will do, you will likely underestimate or write off what that person will actually do.

"I have to let things happen in the framework I have established," Huppert says, "and if I don't, it won't be any good. If I try to force people to act and not respond spontaneously, you'll smell it a mile away. It's not real and genuine. I have to let things happen, and I have to enjoy that part of the process."

That process, during Huppert's Valentine's Day story, unearthed a gem.

When he interviewed the happy couple, he says, "We just kept talking, and finally the wife said, 'I kept the boxes, and I'm glad I kept him too.' Then she said, 'I like them both.' And then she said, 'No, take that back – I love one of them.'

"And there you go! There's the ending of my story. I couldn't have written that. I couldn't have put those words in her mouth. It's knowing what I need to tell a good story and being patient enough to get those elements, so that I know when I get back to the station that all of the pieces are there. [Then] it's just my job not to screw it up."

Appreciate – and Understand – the Collaborative Experience

Huppert believes wholeheartedly in the power of teamwork and collaboration. When he studied journalism in college, he says, he gravitated towards television because of the opportunity to work every day with a newsgathering partner. He has succeeded as a storyteller, in large part, because of award-winning photographers who bring their own strengths and ideas.

"They make me better than I am," Huppert says. "The secret to my success is having the good sense to work with really good people."

This might feel like a letdown for a solo video journalist who cannot benefit from such collaboration. But you can still learn how traditional crews operate – and then customize those tricks for life on your own.

For example, in the chapter on shooting interviews, I mentioned "The Dance," which is how Huppert describes the nonverbal communication with his photographer while speaking with a subject.

"I know I don't want all of my interview angles to look the same, and I know the photographer is going to have to move around to get the shots," Huppert says. "So we're going to dance. He or she is going to lead, and I'm going to follow. I have to wait until he's set on his tripod and done focusing and then ask my question."

A solo act can use these principles as well – and more efficiently. You do not need to worry about "dancing" with a co-worker. You control the operation. You can decide on your own when to move and change angles during an interview.

You can also, even as a one-person orchestra, seek collaboration in other ways. If, when I receive an assignment, I think of a potentially unusual way to execute it, I often run that idea past a nearby co-worker for feedback.

Finally, you can take comfort in the knowledge that even traditional crews often break apart during certain parts of the process. Huppert, for example, writes his long-form pieces by himself at home – "Newsrooms are the worst places to write," he says – and stays out of his photographers' way while they edit. "They're the experts at editing," he says, "so I let them edit. They're mostly done by the time I look at it, and then we tweak. They agonize over the editing like I agonize over the scripts."

Keep Pushing, Growing, and Getting Better

Each of the above tips applies largely to the day-to-day storytelling process. But I could not speak with such a distinguished journalist without asking his advice on how to improve on a grander scale. Huppert responded with a variety of insights, nearly all of which seemed to boil down to two words:

Don't stop.

"Don't ever feel like you're good enough," Huppert said. "I don't feel like I'm someone who came into this with a ton of writing talent. Again, I grew up on a dairy farm in Wisconsin. I just feel like it's effort. It's knowing what your goals are. It's having mentors that will help you along the way. And it's never giving up on your goals."

Huppert specifically advocated seeking chances to learn outside the newsroom.

"Challenge yourself to find avenues for continuing education," he said. "I have done some teaching in Europe. In the Scandinavian countries, they are entitled to a week of learning as journalists. We don't have that here. No one's like, 'It's your week to get your training.' You really have to do that on your own and realize the value.

"Do we seek avenues for continuing education? Some of us do, but most of us don't. We don't say, 'I'm gonna take a week of vacation and pay for a workshop with my own money because it's an investment in my career.'

"Get better at your skills. Go to a workshop. Spend that money to enter the Murrow Awards or your state AP awards. Get known that way. I think sometimes people stop short of where they should be, and they leave themselves in bad situations. Just get good. Get good at something, to the point that you're going to get noticed by someone."

Huppert speaks with the passion of someone who has not yet gotten noticed, let alone received mountains of awards and honors. But he understands that, in this industry, decision makers respond more than anything to results. They might notice effort, and they might notice passion, but above all they notice production. Any journalist looking to get a big break should start by getting to work.

"And," Huppert concludes, "if you're not getting noticed, you're not good enough yet. You have more work to do."

Challenge accepted.

Thinking Big

12

Figure 12.1

Credit: Matt Pearl

We never quite know who will enter our lives and make an everlasting difference.

Who knows where you might meet your spouse? Who knows what will lead to your most rewarding friendships? And who knows who will give you the advice or inspiration that immediately changes how you view your career?

I, for example, did not expect my very first journalism professor to provide me, in one class, with the most important lesson I have ever received about the vocation.

The professor? Richard Schwarzlose.

The class? History and Issues of Journalism.

And the lesson?

Think big.

First-year journalism students at Northwestern rarely knew, when they entered Professor Schwarzlose's class, what they would experience. But when the professor walked in, he instantly captivated the room. A newspaper reporter during the late 1950s and early 1960s, Schwarzlose had since become the journalism school's most tenured professor. When I met him he was in his 60s and still sparkled with enthusiasm.

In his class, he presented us neophytes with on-the-job scenarios that would challenge our ethical beliefs. He addressed these scenarios to individual students and questioned us, Socratic-method style, until we all realized the complexity of the field we wished to enter. Schwarzlose portrayed journalism as a grand, difficult, frustrating, yet rewarding field that required its stewards to take it extremely seriously.

In other words, he portrayed journalism as exactly what it is – or, at least, what it should be.

In this final chapter of the book, I want to instill that message within you.

Unfortunately, the very nature of the news industry often pushes journalists to think small. We are told we must "feed the beast" of daily news, churning out stories based more on immediacy than long-term importance. We rarely have the time within a day to think about a story beyond its basic execution. On a larger scale, we seldom get the chance to think about our careers beyond our day-to-day work.

I implore you to think big.

Think big about your stories. How can each one be unique? What are the societal factors and larger issues that affect an individual news event?

Think big about your career. Where do you want to be five years from now? Ten years from now? Thirty years from now? What do you truly want to accomplish?

Think long-term, large-scale, and beyond what's right in front of you.

Think big.

Here are nine pieces of advice that will help in that quest.

Evaluate Your Work with an Objective Eye

During the daily grind in which you must constantly juggle various tasks, you might struggle to find time for any extra steps that don't directly aid the completion of your work.

But you need to make time.

In the previous chapter, Boyd Huppert spoke of the importance of continual education outside of the newsroom. You can apply that concept to your stories as well, analyzing them as often as possible to learn where you need the least and most improvement.

Every weekend I give myself the following assignment: I choose two of my stories from the past week, watch them, and critique them. I try to be as honest as possible, putting myself in the place of my audience and asking if I satisfied their needs. I write down my thoughts: Where did I succeed? Where did I falter? How could I have approached the story differently, both with and without the benefit of hindsight?

This step, for me, often produces immediate dividends. I encourage you to try to improve a little bit every day. You will likely be surprised, when you look back a year later, by how much you have grown.

Seek Feedback and Critiques from Others

Of course, you should never rely solely on your own evaluation. You should try to gather as many valued opinions as you can find.

But you likely won't receive those opinions unless you seek them out.

During my first decade in the business, I can recall a mere handful of times when managers or colleagues reached out to me with large-scale feedback. I have tried to make a habit of reaching out to them, usually sitting down with a manager every few months to gain some guidance. Perhaps this is a daring move. By setting such a meeting, I open myself to managerial criticism. But I view it as a way to find out if I am achieving what they expect of me. I also value the chance to receive the thoughts of someone who watches my work nearly as much as I do.

But I don't stop with my employers. I seek the comments of those outside the industry. Ultimately, we exist to serve our audience, and we should always take steps to ensure we connect with them. As you develop in the business – and even after you feel you have developed – I urge you to reach out to whomever you can, from family and friends to Facebook followers.

They will likely notice something you would never have expected.

Don't Be Afraid to Ask for Help

This piece of advice is targeted specifically at solo video journalists. Younger ones often feel they must live up to their job descriptions of handling assignments entirely by themselves. In doing so, they forget a fundamental fact:

They still belong to a newsroom. And the decision makers in that newsroom want them to produce strong stories.

Even as a solo act, you can and should take advantage of the resources in your building. If you are driving but need to look up an important phone number, call an assignment editor. If you truly need a photographer because of the nature of your story, reach out and ask for one.

I, for example, must occasionally cover a hearing at a federal courthouse, where I cannot carry my camera or even my cell phone. The photographer in me must leave all of my gear in the car while the reporter in me sits in court. Then, when the hearing concludes, I must scramble back to the car (usually parked five minutes away), grab my camera, rush back to the courthouse, and hope to catch the various newsmakers in the story before they leave.

This, as you can see, is a logistical nightmare. I make sure my bosses realize this before they send me.

I like to think I have built trust and respect with my news managers. Because they see my effort, time management, and productivity as a one-person crew, they take seriously my requests for help. They cannot always provide it – sometimes they simply cannot spare a photographer, even for federal court – but they usually try. You should not feel shy, when necessary, about asking.

Be Willing to Stand up for Yourself

Similarly, if you feel you consistently do not receive the necessary support from your newsroom, you should not hesitate to speak up.

Let me be blunt: very few managers and producers truly grasp the solo experience. They might understand it on a basic level – we do the jobs of two traditional journalists – but they do not necessarily realize the complications, subtleties, and challenges that arise on a daily basis.

This means you will sometimes need to be your loudest advocate. Do you feel at risk covering a story by yourself in a dangerous area? Have you been asked to do something that's doable for a two-person crew but physically impossible for a crew of one? Let someone know.

For a long time in my career, I took a stand against solo live shots, particularly in outdoor environments. They required more equipment than I could carry at once. They also required so much set-up time that they detracted from my ability to report. Beyond that, they generally seemed patently unsafe as a one-person operation, a sentiment shared by many in the MMJ Survey discussed in Chapter 10.

These days, one-person live shots have become easier to execute, thanks to stronger technology in far smaller and more portable devices. But I still rarely recommend doing them alone, particularly at stations that possess the resources to do otherwise. I speak up when I find myself in a vulnerable situation, and you should prepare to do the same.

Be Ready and Willing to Adapt to Change

You should also prepare to not get too comfortable.

I have mentioned this in previous chapters, but I must reiterate: TV news constantly tests its employees' ability to evolve with the business. One need look no further than the rise of MMJs. For a long time, they did not exist, save for a select few reporters in the smallest of markets. But as the equipment has become more manageable – and as stations' budgets have tightened – managers nationwide have warmed to the concept.

The industry will continue to change, and anyone entering TV news should be prepared to change with it. Just as great journalists refuse to approach stories with a pre-written script, you should develop long-term goals but not be bound to them. Expect to face unpredictability, and be willing to embrace it.

Establish and Understand Larger Goals for Your Career

But don't let such unpredictability affect your ability to think big.

Very few people wander into the field of journalism. They seek it out, accompanied by grand aspirations of how they might use the power of the press to change the world.

Then they enter the business and lose sight of those goals amidst a grueling, jaded culture.

I have met too many journalists who allow themselves to be defined – and assigned – by their employers. But I have also met many who possess clear long-term goals and actively work to incorporate them into their short-term jobs. They reach out to their managers with story ideas or larger objectives, and they often – if they prove worthy – receive previously unforeseen opportunities.

I urge you to think seriously about what you wish to accomplish in this business. You cannot chart your own path if you do not know what you want it to be. If your larger goals do not fit into the stereotypical news box, you should feel even more compelled to pursue them. Local news exists in a growing state of monotony. So many anchors and reporters sound the same, look the same, and tell stories the same. We desperately need people who are willing to break that pattern.

Simply put, do not be afraid to aim for what does not yet exist.

Aim high, and figure out how to work toward your goals in your current situation. Then check in repeatedly on your progress. Do not let those dreams drift away.

Find Role Models and Mentors to Remind You of Your Goals

And don't try to reach your dreams without help.

I was fortunate in my young life to find mentorship without truly prioritizing it. I mentioned Professor Schwarzlose, who became my advisor in college and nurtured my journalistic growth throughout my time at Northwestern. But I can name several people, from high school thorough the early stages of my career, who both championed my development and inspired me with their work. I have always valued their influence, and today I try to be as helpful as I can to aspiring journalists with big goals. (That's largely why I wrote this book!)

That said, I only realized the value of mentorship in retrospect, and I wish I had placed more emphasis on it earlier. I encourage young journalists to seek out those influences, especially in a climate where connecting is easier than ever. If you know someone whose guidance you wish to obtain, you can probably find that person's work e-mail address or social media accounts within seconds.

What makes a great mentor? That differs for each person, but I have always found value in someone who: (a) has been in the business longer than me, (b) has seen success similar to that I wish for myself, and (c) is as willing to offer guidance as I am to receive it. Remember: even as a solo act, you will not succeed in this business without others' help. You should not feel hesitant to ask.

Maintain Your Enthusiasm; Maintain Your Effort

Journalism is a field that benefits the grinders.

Those who put in extra time and take extra steps always seem to gain a giant advantage over their peers. They cultivate sources, chase story ideas, and cherish each assignment as an opportunity – even if, to do so, they must stay a little later and work a little longer.

That mentality is difficult to sustain if you don't love what you're doing.

Sadly, journalism is also a field where those who lose their passion can really struggle. The business can be upsetting, disturbing, and even dangerous. It can, with frightening speed, turn idealists into cynics.

I always encourage aspiring journalists to think deeply before dedicating their young adult lives to this profession. For my first job, I moved to a small city and worked 60-hour weeks. I struggled in some ways with the transition, but I would have struggled far more had I not loved my work. I threw extraordinary energy into a position that demanded it, and I became a stronger journalist.

You will likely need to make similar sacrifices throughout your career. For that reason, I always impart the following to those who ask my advice about entering the industry:

Know the business and the lifestyle it brings. And be sure you possess the passion to both navigate that business and be great within it.

Always Remember: Life Comes First

My final piece of advice is perhaps the least relevant to life as a solo video journalist. It is perhaps the most relevant to life in general:

Your career isn't everything.

Even as a still relatively young journalist, I have experienced some of the industry's most extraordinary highs: winning national awards, interviewing icons, and covering some of the world's biggest events. But I have experienced even greater joys outside of work: traveling to foreign countries, serving in my community, developing meaningful friendships, and, most recently, getting married to my love and welcoming our daughters.

Despite the temptation to consume myself with my job – a temptation to which I have occasionally succumbed, particularly earlier in my career – I have always tried to keep in mind the many other amazing gifts of life in this world. I did not hear this advice enough in my college years, but I impress it upon those who seek my perspective.

Before you enter the field, you should be aware of all it brings – much of it positive. You will meet a wide range of individuals, travel all around the regions in which you work, and gain access to events, places, and people unreachable to most. More than anything, you will possess the power and tools to present important stories to a mass audience – one that extends, thanks to social media, beyond traditional borders.

But you will also face erratic schedules. You will work long and often abnormal hours, from morning and late-night shifts to weekends and holidays. You will not get paid much, particularly in your early years. Above all, you will work in a field whose future is entirely unpredictable – a quality that may seem more attractive in your 20s than in your 30s, 40s, and 50s.

I encourage you to think of the many goals for your life and determine how they mesh with a career in journalism. Many in the field disparage the concept of work–life balance, but I champion it. I view work–life balance as a critical component to one's happiness, and I urge you to constantly consider it as you make major career decisions.

Most of all, I simply wish you the best. I have seen firsthand the joys of working in journalism, particularly as a solo video journalist, and I yearn to see that joy in others. I hope you have found this book beneficial and enlightening, and I encourage you – one last time – to follow the lesson I learned years ago from Professor Schwarzlose:

Think big.

Now go get 'em.

Index

Made in the USA
Monee, IL
24 January 2023

26063404R00111